WHITE NIGHTS VOYAGE

From Moscow to St Petersburg

D1300788

Text:

Nikita Krivtsov

Photographs:

Victor Gritsyuk

White Nights Voyage
From Moscow to St Petersburg

ISBN: 1 871489 23 7

Distributed in the Russian Federation by
Jupiter Joint Stock Co.
Petrovka ul. 8/11
Moscow 103031

Design:
Gane Aleksic

Art Editor:
Tom Wilson

Editors:
Victor Firsov
Madge Phillips

Translators:
Cynthia Carlile
Margarita Kvartskhava

Cover picture: Folk dance festival on Kizhi Island, Lake Onega

Typesetting by Communicating Ltd, London

Organisation by Eurocity Associates, London

Printed and bound in Slovenia by
Tiskarna Ljudska Pravica, Ljubljana

CONTENTS

p. 5

'FROM THE VARANGIANS TO THE GREEKS'
Land of the White Nights. Moscow Canal. Kimry.
Kalyazin. Uglich. Rybinsk Reservoir. Cherepovets.
Along the Sheksna. Northern Dvina System.

p. 37

CYRIL AND FERAPONT
Goritsi. Cyril-Belozero Monastery and Kirillov.
Ferapont Monastery. Belozersk and the White Lake.

p. 84

SAILING TO KIZHI
Vytegra. The Canals. Lake Onega. Kizhi Island.
Wooden Churches and Chapels. Village Life and Homesteads.

p. 112

ALONG THE SVIR RIVER
Petrozavodsk. The Svir River. Podporozhie.
Villages of the Podporozhie Silver Ring.
Yuksovichi. Gems of Wooden Architecture.
Lodeinoe Pole. Monastery of St Alexander of the Svir.

p. 131

THE HOLY ISLAND
Lake Ladoga and Valaam Island. Valaam Monastery.
Old and New Ladoga. Schliesselburg and the Neva.

p. 144
MAP OF THE REGION

'FROM THE VARANGIANS TO THE GREEKS'

1. The clock on the Spasskaya Tower of the Moscow Kremlin is the main clock in Russia by which time is set throughout the country. The Spasskaya Tower and the chimes of the Kremlin clock have thus become the symbol not only of Moscow, but of all Russia.

The Land of the White Nights, the north-western region of European Russia, and its capital, St Petersburg, are easily reached from Moscow by overnight train or a day's journey by car, but to discover more about this area, it is far more rewarding to take the route used by traders many centuries ago. Following major Russian rivers, lakes and canals, this 'way from the Varangians (Vikings) to the Greeks' led from the Baltic along the Volga and the Dnieper rivers to the Caspian and Black seas. Travelling by this same route, albeit in the opposite direction, from Moscow to St Petersburg, we arrive in the Land of the White Nights, with its grandly austere, yet romantic landscapes and its scattered villages that have preserved many elements of the traditional way of life. Here, too, are historic towns, old monasteries and churches, similar in style, yet each with its own unique character.

North-western Russia includes the territory of the regions of Tver (covering an area of 84,100 sq. km.), Yaroslavl (36,400 sq. km.), Vologda (145,000 sq. km.) and Leningrad (85,900 sq. km.), and the Republic of Karelia (172,400 sq. km.).

Though this area of the country is predominantly low-lying, hills and numerous moraine ridges left by glaciers give variety to the landscape. In fact, the northern shores of Lake Ladoga and Lake Onega are so rocky that they are reminiscent of Scandinavia.

The north-western part of Russia is intersected by many rivers, and it is along the largest of these—the Volga, the Sheksna, the Svir and the Neva—that vessels ply between Moscow and St Petersburg. The region is also famous for its innumerable lakes (another legacy of the ice age), among them the two biggest fresh water lakes in Europe: Ladoga and Onega. It was this abundance of rivers and lakes, and the difficulties of traversing the forested, marshy countryside, that led to the development of water transport in this part of Russia through a network of interconnected waterways.

Karelia, lying between the White Sea and Onega and Ladoga, has more than 60,000 lakes on its territory. Finland, famous throughout the world as a land of lakes, has 151 lakes for every 1,000 sq. km. of land. Karelia has 350! Half the territory of this republic is covered by forests, while another 18 per cent is marshland. The mixed forests of the Upper Volga basin give way, further north, to conifers: in Karelia there is true taiga of the Siberian type. Of the other territories, the most heavily wooded are Vologda Region and the areas around the Svir River.

In comparison with its area, the population of the North-west is very small: Tver Region—1.7 million, Yaroslavl Region—1.5 million, Vologda Region—1.3 million, Leningrad Region—1.5 million, excluding St Petersburg (or 6.5 million including St Petersburg), and Karelia— 800,000. Most of the population in this territory are ethnic Russians, though in Karelia and the Tver, Leningrad and Vologda regions there are also Karelians and Veps, who belong to the Finno-Ugric group of peoples. The Karelians, the second largest ethnic group in the Republic of Karelia (80,000 people), are also to be found living in compact groups in Tver Region, to which they emigrated in the 17th century from Karelia when it was occupied by the Swedes. The Veps, whose language is related to that of the Karelians, are one of the smallest ethnic groups in Russia, numbering less than 10,000. They live mainly in Leningrad Region, to the south of the Svir River, on the Karelian side of Lake Onega to the south of Petrozavodsk, particularly around the village of Sholtozero, and also in Vologda Region.

2. The Kremlin, Moscow. The rise of the city, founded in 1147 on the banks of the Moskva River, owed much to its central geographical position and its location on important river trade routes: south along the Moskva and then down the Oka and Volga to the Caspian Sea, and north, via portage, to the rivers flowing into the Baltic.

The Finno-Ugric tribes, once the core population of north-western Russia, were gradually overrun by Slavic tribes and assimilated. That the Veps, known in old Russia as 'Ves', once inhabited a far larger area is revealed not only by old chronicles and popular legends, but also by the names of towns such as Vesegonsk (Ves Yegonskaya), and Cherepovets (Cherepo-Ves) on the shores of the Rybinsk Reservoir.

Although some of the towns in this area were founded in the very early days of the creation of the Russian state, most of them remained for many centuries remote outposts in a sparsely populated territory. Indeed, even in the last century Karelia was seen as 'the metropolitan Siberia' because of its virgin forests and harsh climate, and also because it was used as a place of exile from St Petersburg. At various times princes and ecclesiastics who had fallen into disfavour, as well as political dissidents, were exiled to the fortresses and monasteries of north-western Russia. In the 17th century, Patriarch Nikon, renowned for his church reforms, was stripped of his post and imprisoned in the Ferapont Monastery and then the Cyril-Belozero Monastery, while at the end of the 16th century the eighth and last wife of Ivan the Terrible passed away the remainder of her days in Uglich and Goritsi.

Because of its remoteness on the periphery of the country, north-western Russia was chosen down the centuries as a site for monasteries. On the one hand, the monks were able to find solitude here, while, on the other, the monastic communities also served as outposts through which the central government spread its influence.

While northern Russia was little affected by the Tatar invasion which devastated the whole of the central region and left it in vassalage for several centuries, it felt the impact of other wars and invasions. It was here, particularly in the present Leningrad Region and Karelia, that Russia and its neighbours were in constant conflict to secure access to the Baltic. In 1240, on the banks of the Neva, Prince Alexander and his forces won fame by blocking the path of the Swedish army. After this victory, the prince was known as Alexander Nevsky (of the Neva). A couple of years later, on the ice of Lake Chudskoe, he triumphed over the Teutonic Knights in a battle which has gone down in history as the Battle on the Ice, brilliantly recreated by Eisenstein in his film *Alexander Nevsky*. The Russian troops inflicted a crushing defeat on the Germans, assisted by natural forces: the ice cracked under the heavy weight of the armour-clad knights, and they drowned in the freezing waters of the lake.

In the 16th century Ivan the Terrible waged long wars to gain access to the Baltic Sea. The death of the last member of the Rurik dynasty at the end of the century ushered in a period of intrigue, power struggles, civil war and foreign incursions known in Russia as the Time of Troubles. This came to an end in 1613, when Michael, the first of the Romanov dynasty, ascended the throne. In the early 17th century, Polish-Lithuanian and Swedish troops ravaged northern Russia, and very few towns and monasteries survived unscathed.

The territory along the banks of the Neva and the shores of Lake Ladoga constantly changed hands between the Swedes and the Russians, and it was not until the reign of Peter the Great, following the Northern War of 1700-1721, that the lands adjoining the Gulf of Finland finally became part of Russia.

For many years afterwards, this part of the country, which was considered a remote borderland, was spared major social and political upheavals. During the Second World War Karelia and the present Leningrad Region were again overrun by foreign invasion, and many towns, villages and architectural monuments were reduced to ruins. The famous Life Road that ran across the ice of Lake Ladoga was the only link between besieged Leningrad and the rest of the country during the unprecedented nine-hundred-day blockade which the city heroically survived.

The early 19th century saw the creation of a shipping route between St Petersburg and Moscow which stimulated the development of this territory without, however, much altering either its landscape or the lifestyle of its inhabitants. There was no heavy industry in this area, and even the period of the Stalinist five-year plans, which saw the rapid industrialisation of the country, had little impact here. Today, the only industrial centres encountered by tourists sailing from Moscow to St Petersburg are Cherepovets and Petrozavodsk.

For some of the remote areas of this part of Russia, where adequate roads appeared only comparatively recently, water transport remains, as in former times, the main means of communication. Following the last modernisation of the Volga-Baltic navigation route, in the 1950s, the importance of inland water transport rose sharply. Today, this navigation system conveys timber from Karelia, the area around the Svir River and Vologda Region, mineral ores from the Kola Peninsula and northern Karelia, and metal from Cherepovets, not to mention other freight and large numbers of passengers. For towns such as Vytegra or Belozersk, water transport still plays a key role, while Cherepovets and Petrozavodsk have become major ports, the latter even handling overseas shipping.

Thanks to the fact that industrialisation bypassed this region, the

3. With the construction of the Moskva-Volga Canal in 1937, Moscow became a deep-water port directly linked with both the Volga and the northern regions of the country. The Northern River Terminal, built at the same time as the canal, is a typical example of Stalinist architecture.

landscape of rivers, lakes and forests has remained untouched and it is one of the most environmentally-clean areas in the country. The navigation route passes through localities noted for farming, forestry and fisheries. The Karelian side of Lake Ladoga has long been known for its marble and granite, which was used, for example, in the construction of embankments and bridges in St Petersburg. The old mineral mines in Karelia have long since been worked out, and the new ones are considerably further north.

That the North-west remained a remote border territory even in the 20th century has proved to be a blessing: examples of old wooden architecture long since vanished elsewhere have survived here; many old towns and villages have preserved their original appearance, unaf-

4. Some families living beside major rivers have for generations owed their livelihood to water transport. On the Svir, for example, whole dynasties of pilots guided ships through the dangerous rapids. After the construction of the hydro-electric power plants, the rapids disappeared, but shipping is still of economic importance to local communities.

fected by demolition, mindless renovation and mass housing developments; the ancient monasteries suffered far less from the campaigns against religion waged during the years of Soviet government.

The visitor to this region will find some of the oldest Russian towns: Old Ladoga, Belozersk and Uglich, ancient monasteries which were once among the largest, richest and most renowned in the country, such as Cyril-Belozero, Valaam and Alexander of the Svir, and the old Russian fortresses of Oreshek in Schliesselburg, Old Ladoga and Korela in Priozersk. The area around the Svir River and Lake Onega is particularly notable for its wonderful examples of wooden architecture: those on Kizhi Island are already internationally famous, while others are only now becoming better known to the world at large.

5. The myriad rivers, lakes and canals in north-western Russia makes water transport in this region as commonplace as the bus. In some places, boats are the most convenient or even the only means of travel.

6. The arrival and departure of vessels are events that enliven the daily round for the local people in some remote regions of Russia. The boat delivers the mail, food, other goods, and also brings in new faces. The wharf is a window on the outer world, particularly for the elderly and the children of small townships, who always gather on the quay to greet incoming ships.

Many of the places here are linked with the names of Russian tsars and grand dukes—the legendary Rurik in the 9th century, Ivan the Terrible in the 16th century, Peter the Great in the 18th century—and also with one of the greatest icon painters of medieval Russia, Dyonisius. Later, many celebrated Russian painters, writers and poets visited this area.

Though the North-west occupies a relatively small part of Russia (less than four per cent of its territory, inhabited by just over four per cent of the total population), a journey across it gives some idea of the country's past, of much that has been destroyed elsewhere by modern civilisation. The traveller also gains an impression of the beauty and diversity of the land, its vast expanses and broad horizons. There is something traditionally Russian in this journey along the Volga and other Russian rivers and waterways, which combines the pleasures of a voyage of discovery with an opportunity to feel and understand the spirit of the country.

The Moscow Canal linking the capital to the Upper Volga leads due north. The ship completes this part of the voyage overnight, sailing along this waterway which was built in the 1930s and made the city accessible to the largest ships. Moscow thus became 'a port of five seas'—the Caspian, the Sea of Azov, the Black Sea, the Baltic Sea and the White Sea.

First called the Moscow-Volga Canal and renamed in 1947 to mark the 800th anniversary of the founding of the city, the Moscow

7. Kimry: the Saviour Transfiguration Cathedral, now the only functioning church in the town. When it was built in the early 20th century, Kimry had four churches and was an important trade and industrial centre on the Upper Volga.

Canal was constructed to resolve two problems: the capital's growing demand for water and its need for a direct link with the Upper Volga. Interestingly enough, the idea of building this canal, and many others in Russia, first emerged in the reign of Peter the Great, who wanted to establish a direct water link between the old and new capitals. It was then forgotten for a century, until 1817, when Emperor Alexander I thought of raising the grandiose Cathedral of Christ the Saviour to commemorate the victory over Napoleon in 1812. To solve the problem of transporting vast quantities of building materials for what was, in its day, a huge construction project, it was decided to link the Sestra, a tributary of the Dubna River, which flows into the Volga, with the Istra, a tributary of the Moskva River. Work began in 1825, and the construction of this nine-kilometre-long canal with 41 locks continued for nineteen years. However, the canal had a very limited capacity, being able to handle barges with cargoes of 35 tons at most. After the completion of the railway line between Moscow and St Petersburg, the canal began to fall into disuse, and in 1860 it was abandoned altogether.

Today, the canal is 128 kilometres long, of which 20 kilometres is

8. Kalyazin: the 70-metre-high belfry (built in 1800 by a local architect) is all that remains of the St Nicholas Cathedral, demolished prior to the creation of the Uglich Reservoir. The belfry survived only because it was planned to use it as a light-house.

taken up by water reservoirs. There are nine locks, in which ships are raised to a height of 38 metres above the level of the Volga and 36 metres above the level of the Moskva River.

By road, the distance between Moscow and the Volga (130 km.) can be covered in less than three hours. The journey by local train to the town of Kimry (Savelovo station) also takes three hours.

Kimry, a town of some 60,000 inhabitants on the Upper Volga in Tver Region, was formerly a typical Volga trading and crafts settlement. However, it gained distinction and became known throughout Russia thanks to its skilled shoemakers. This craft brought the settlement prosperity, and in the 19th century the local merchants built a magnificent hostelry in the pseudo-Russian style, a market centre and—surprisingly in a small provincial town—multi-storey apartment buildings with art nouveau ornamentation.

Of the tall churches in Kimry, only the Ascension Church, built in 1813, is still standing, its belfry dominating the town. There is also a local ethnography museum of some interest, one of the oldest on the

Upper Volga, founded in 1918.

At the beginning of this century, when it grew to the size of a town, Kimry continued to specialise in footwear. During the Soviet period, a considerable number of Vietnamese worked in the shoe factory. Though demand for their labour in this area has fallen, many of them have nonetheless remained in Kimry and have taken up small-scale trading. The townsfolk are quite happy to buy footwear from them, and also other goods brought in from China, countries of Southeast Asia, and elsewhere.

Kalyazin, a little further down the Volga, can be reached from Moscow by train (from Savelovsky Terminal) or by car via Sergiev Posad (169 km.). The hydrofoils linking Uglich, Kimry and Tver also stop here. Built on hills divided by a broad expanse of water, Kalyazin is in many ways a typical town of the Upper Volga, but it, too, has a claim to distinction: half of the old town lies under water! When the series of Upper Volga dams were built in the 1930s, the level of the Volga rose, flooding the low-lying settlements along its banks. Some villages and towns disappeared completely. The tall belfry of the St Nicholas Cathedral (built in 1800), rising out of the water in the middle of the river, has become one of the sights of Kalyazin. Large cruise boats do not stop here, but the belfry, around which a tiny island was backfilled in the 1980s, can be clearly seen for a long time from the deck of a passing boat.

Like Sergiev Posad (Zagorsk), now in suburban Moscow, Kalyazin was for a long time a 'monastery town' which developed from craft and trading settlements clustered around the old and wealthy Trinity Monastery, founded in the 15th century. The monastery and the town, which was granted civic status in 1775, acquired their name of Kalyazin from the local estate-owner, Kalyaga. The 16th-century monastery church also disappeared under the water, but its 17th-century frescoes were removed from the walls: some are now kept at the Museum of Architecture in Moscow, and some in the ethnography museum in Kalyazin.

Uglich in Yaroslavl Region, on the right bank of the Volga, is where ships sailing from Moscow to St Petersburg make their first stop (after a journey of just under 24 hours). It can also be reached by train from Moscow (six hours) and by road via Rostov (283 km.) or Kalyazin (229 km.).

The Uglich chronicles link the founding of the town to a certain Prince Jan Pleskovich (or Pskovich, a native of Pskov), who was sent to this area by Grand Duke Igor 'in order to collect tribute'. The arrival of his force is dated to 937, when Jan Pleskovich built his first fortification at the spot where the Kamennaya stream flows into the Volga. The name of Uglich is first mentioned in the Ipatiev Chronicle in 1148, at which time the town was part of the principality of Rostov. Around 1218 Uglich became the seat of a small regional apanage (land endowed upon a ruler's younger son), under Prince Vladimir, grandson of Grand Duke Vsevolod the Big Nest.

In the winter of 1238, Tatar hordes invaded north-eastern Russia, and at the end of the 13th century, during one of their attacks, the town was sacked; Uglich and the surrounding area remained desolate for many years. In 1328, Prince Ivan Danilovich annexed the town to Moscow, and from that time onwards Uglich came under the Muscovite princes. Prince Dmitry Donskoi, who inflicted the first defeat on the Tatars in the battle of the Kulikovo Field in 1380, attached great

11. Detail of the fresco 'The Slaying of Tsarevich Dmitry', a rare example of an historical painting in a religious building. The story is presented in a series of film-like scenes: the dressing of the Tsarevich, his murder, the weeping Tsaritsa and Dmitry's nurse, the citizens attacking and killing the assassins, messengers riding to Moscow, and the body of Dmitry being conveyed to the capital. The composition concludes with a panorama of the Moscow Kremlin and an image of the Tsarevich depicted as a saint.

importance to Uglich as a Volga frontier town of the Moscow principality. In 1375 he rebuilt the fortress and founded the first monastery, dedicated to the Assumption of the Virgin (later known as the Alexeevsky Monastery).

The 14th century saw the beginning of the unification of Russian lands around Moscow, and from this time onwards the history of Uglich is closely bound up with that of Muscovy. In the 15th century the town was in the ascendant, although it continued to be one of the centres of internecine strife. In 1446, Prince Vassily II of Moscow, who was waging war against Prince Yuri Dmitrievich of Galich and Dmitry Yurievich Shemiaka, was seized and blinded (as a result of which he was nicknamed 'the Dark'), and then exiled with his family to Uglich. Later, with the help of his supporters, Vassily the Dark succeeded in recovering his throne, and then pillaged the town where he had spent his exile. His son, Andrei, later called 'the Big', was born

12. The Church of Dmitry contains a unique relic: the bell dating from the 15th-16th century which was used to raise the alarm and inform the people of the death of the Tsarevich.

here in Uglich. He became the apanage prince of Uglich, and it was during this period, in the second half of the 15th century, that the apanage principality of Uglich and its main town enjoyed their greatest prosperity. New fortified walls were built around the town, together with a palace and a magnificent cathedral in the Intercession Monastery; several monasteries were also founded in the surroundings.

At the end of the 16th century there occurred in Uglich a mysterious and tragic event which had an impact on Russian history and has often been depicted in Russian art. In the spring of 1584, following the death of Ivan the Terrible, his youngest son, Tsarevich Dmitry, was sent to Uglich together with his widowed mother, Tsaritsa Maria Nagaya, and a large retinue. On May 15, 1591, the Tsarevich, the last representative of the Rurik dynasty, died. According to the official version, he was playing with a knife and fell on it by accident, but the Tsaritsa levelled an accusation of murder against men in the service of Boris

19

Godunov, a nobleman who was intriguing for the throne. On hearing this, the residents of Uglich rose up and killed the accused men. A special commission of enquiry, headed by Prince Vassily Shuisky, arrived in Uglich and decided that 'the death of Tsarevich Dmitry was an act of God' in the form of an attack of epilepsy. As for the townsfolk who had slain the men in Godunov's service, they were accused of 'treason' and harshly punished; many were executed, others imprisoned or exiled to Siberia. Maria Nagaya herself was charged with having failed to keep due watch over her son and forced to take the veil. Such was the end of the ancient dynasty of Russian rulers which traced its lineage back to the 9th century and the legendary Rurik, founder of Kievan Rus.

However, this was only the beginning of a series of tragic events which were to follow. In 1601, an impostor appeared in Poland claiming to be Tsarevich Dmitry and appealed to the Polish king for help in 'recovering his father's throne'. In 1605, taking advantage of the peasant war and treachery by the Muscovite nobility, who turned against the tsar, Boris Godunov, the false Dmitry and his Polish troops entered Moscow. Less than a year later, the boyars killed the impostor during a popular uprising in Moscow, and put Vassily Shuisky on the throne. He announced that Tsarevich Dmitry had been killed on the orders of Boris Godunov and had him canonised as a martyr. The mortal remains of the Tsarevich were brought to Moscow and placed in the Archangel Cathedral in the Kremlin.

Soon another impostor showed up, and at the end of 1608 Uglich was taken by the forces of the second false Dmitry, but the local residents drove them out. The Poles threatened the town on several occasions thereafter, but it was not until the spring of 1611 that they seized

14. Uglich: the Church of the Nativity of St John the Baptist 'on the Volga' (1689-1690). This is also linked with a tragic event: the abduction and murder of the son of Nikofor Chepolosov, a wealthy local leather merchant, who paid for the construction of the church as a burial place for his son.

15. The dome of the Church of the Nativity of St John the Baptist.

and burnt the town after a traitor had opened the fortress gates for them.

Gradually the town was rebuilt and recovered its former grandeur. Uglich merchants once again appeared on the river trade routes of the Russian North. Between 1660 and 1664, the walls of the fortress were rebuilt and numerous churches erected, along with the Resurrection Monastery.

With the launching of the Petrine reforms in the 18th century, when an imperial decree prohibited the construction of stone buildings in provincial towns—all stone was to go to building the new capital of St Petersburg—construction of large buildings was suspended for some time. Although a plan regulating the urban development of Uglich was passed in 1784, it remained a typical old-Russian provincial town. In the 1780s the dilapidated and no longer necessary fortress was dismantled, and in the early 19th century the earthen ramparts around the trading settlement were flattened. In the mid-19th century quite a few buildings in the classical style appeared in the town.

The Uglich of the 19th century was a quiet district town. With the creation of the Mariinsky Volga-Baltic navigation system, traffic along the Volga to St Petersburg went via Rybinsk, bypassing Uglich. Many local residents began to leave their homes to look for jobs in larger cities.

At the end of the 1930s, the Uglich electric power station was built, one of the first on the chain of Volga dams. The Intercession Monastery with its monuments dating from the 15th to 17th centuries was blown up, and its ruins disappeared beneath the water. By the 1960s, half the churches had been demolished and the walls of existing monasteries dismantled, impairing the architectural integrity of the town.

Despite these depredations, Uglich, with its population of 60,000, has retained numerous architectural and historical monuments and its

16. The Saviour Transfiguration Cathedral (1713-1716) in the Uglich Kremlin, which combined traditional Russian architecture with features characteristic of the early 18th century. In 1984, specialists from the Uglich watch factory installed an electronic clock in the belfry. Now the town hears its melodic chimes every half hour.

atmosphere of bygone centuries, along with the traditions and lifestyle of a typical Russian provincial town.

Sightseeing in Uglich usually begins with the fortress or Kremlin, on the banks of the Volga, where the majority of the historical and architectural monuments of the town are concentrated. In former times almost every old Russian town had its kremlin (*kreml*) or fortress, its walls encompassing the central section. In Uglich the Kremlin itself has gone, but the name is still used to designate the oldest part of the town, occupying a peninsula on the banks of the Volga between the two streams, the Kamennaya and the Shelkovka. Only the moats, one of which has become a picturesque pond, now remain of the Kremlin fortifications.

The oldest structure on the territory of the former Kremlin is the Chamber of the palace of the apanage princes, just a small part of the great palace complex built by Prince Andrei the Big in the 1480s. The Chamber, some ten years older than the Faceted Palace in the Moscow Kremlin, is of exceptional interest since only a few secular buildings

17. Uglich: the Epiphany
Convent with churches dedicated to the Smolensk Virgin
(1689-1700) and the Fedorov
Virgin (1818). The former, the
oldest building in the convent,
underwent several alterations,
but through restoration work its
roof has regained its original
appearance: covered with
gleaming green tiles.

18, 19. The Church of St John
the Baptist of the Alekseevsky
Monastery (1681), typical of
Uglich architecture in the last
quarter of the 17th century. In
contrast to the neighbouring
Divnaya Church, which soars
upwards, the five-domed church
appears low and squat.

20. The Assumption or Divnaya
Church of the Alekseevsky
Monastery (1628), a rare example of a triple hip-roofed
church.

21. Kamenny Ruchei (overleaf).
At the spot where this stream
joins the Volga a fortress was
built in 937, around which the
town of Uglich then developed.

in Russia have survived from this period. The palace complex once included living quarters, auxiliary buildings and defence structures, all enclosed within a brick wall stretching along the river bank. The excavated remains of these buildings can be seen.

The palace itself was destroyed during the Polish invasion. The Chamber, severely damaged by fire, was left in ruins for a long time, and ran the risk of being dismantled for bricks, as happened with the old church and most of the palace. In 1801, the merchant A. Kozhevnikov repaired the building, and at the end of the last century it was further restored to mark the third centenary of the death of Tsarevich Dmitry. The Uglich Museum of Russian Antiquities has been housed inside the palace Chamber since 1892.

Another monument in the Uglich Kremlin connected with the death of the Tsarevich is the Church of Dmitry 'on the Blood', raised on the site of his murder on the very edge of the Volga River. This memorial to the last of the Rurik dynasty was built on the orders of Peter and Johann Alexeevich in 1692 at the expense of Princess

22. The Sheksna River, mentioned by this name in chronicles as early as 1071. It was along the Sheksna that Russians penetrated northwards, particularly into the region around Lake Beloe.

Cherkasskaya, a relative of the deceased Tsaritsa Maria Nagaya. The church has five domes, a refectory and belfry—a style popular in 17th-century Moscow. The interior walls are covered with interesting frescoes, among them the large composition on the western wall, 'The Slaying of Tsarevich Dmitry' (1772), a rare example of a historical painting inside a church. Among the works on the gilded iconostasis is the Tsarevich Dmitry icon, an exact copy of the lost original.

The unusual bier covered with oriental brocade in front of the iconostasis was used to carry the body of the Tsarevich to Moscow. His remains were returned to Uglich in 1630, when the first wooden church was built where the present stone church now stands.

The largest building in the Kremlin area is the Saviour Transfiguration Cathedral (1713-1716), with a 37-metre belfry (1730) in the Naryshkin baroque style beside it. Its glittering gilded dome, visible for many miles, is a feature typical of the church architecture of the Upper Volga. The interior of the cathedral is decorated with more than fifty fresco compositions painted in the early years of the last

23. The Sheksna River, a trade route which linked the White Sea and the Volga, remains to this day an important transport artery of northern Russia. The rapids near Goritsi that once created difficulties for shipping disappeared following the construction of the Cherepovets hydro-electric power station.

century in the style of the late Renaissance and baroque: 'The Transfiguration with the Scene of the Healing of the Lepers' is, in fact, a copy of a work by Raphael. The cathedral also has a fine collection of icons dating from the 15th to 18th centuries located in the northern side chapel and the western porch. The 16th-century icon of the Intercession of the Virgin was particularly venerated by the citizens of Uglich, and was carried in procession around the town. The collection also includes a 17th-century icon of Tsarevich Dmitry, one of the most memorable images of the tsarevich-saint in icon painting. Examples of 17th-century embroidery from local workshops and the work of local silversmiths are also displayed.

The Epiphany Church (1827), which resembles a secular building more than a church, houses an exhibition of paintings and applied art from the 18th to early 20th century.

The Resurrection Monastery, to the west of the town centre, is known to have existed at the end of the 14th century. The present large stone buildings were erected between 1674 and 1677 and constitute a single architectural ensemble. Regrettably, the monastery has now lost its former majestic appearance. In 1764, it became an ordinary parish church, and in the early 19th century its walls were dismantled.

Next to the Resurrection Monastery, but closer to the Volga, standing almost at the river's edge, is the Church of the Nativity of John the Baptist 'on the Volga', which resembles the Church of Dmitry 'on the Blood', except that it has several additional side chapels and is somewhat more lavishly ornamented with coloured tiles.

24. Cloth dolls are among the souvenirs which can be acquired while travelling through the Land of the White Nights. Made by local craftsmen and brought to the quay to meet incoming tourist boats, they are unlikely to be found anywhere else.

In the centre of the old part of the town stands the Epiphany Convent, founded at the end of the 14th century by Grand Duchess Yevdokia, wife of Dmitry Donskoi. Originally the convent was within the Uglich Kremlin, but in the mid-17th century 'due to cramped conditions', it was transferred outside its walls. The oldest surviving monastery building is the Church of the Smolensk Virgin (1689-1700). To the east of this stands the Church of the Fedorov Virgin (1818). The last building in the ensemble is the huge, five-domed Epiphany Church, erected between 1843 and 1853 to a design by the famous Russian architect Konstantin Ton, who designed the Grand Kremlin Palace and the Cathedral of Christ the Saviour in Moscow.

On the other side of the Kamennaya, on a hill once known as Ogneva Gora, stands the Alekseevsky Monastery. Among its few surviving buildings is the Assumption Church, also known as Divnaya (Wonderful), one of the best-known and most interesting examples of the architecture of the day, which is mentioned in virtually every work on Russian stone architecture. The monastery was founded in 1371 by Metropolitan Alexy on the site of a former pagan temple. Around 1584, a church dedicated to Metropolitan Alexy was built in the monastery—this is the oldest stone building in Uglich outside the Kremlin area. In the 19th and 20th centuries, however, it underwent considerable reconstruction and lost its original appearance. In 1628 the father superior of the monastery completed the Assumption Church, a memorial to those who defended the town during the Time of Troubles. This rare example of a church with three hip roofs was

25. Lake Siverskoe. In Russian villages, the washing is still done in rivers and small lakes, as in the past. The only difference is that today the women sometimes wear rubber gloves in winter.

26. Goritsi Convent was founded in 1544, although its not particularly impressive walls date from the first half of the 19th century. The convent, one of the most remote in the country, was for long a placed of exile for discarded wives and troublesome female relatives of the tsars and princes.

regarded as one of the most beautiful and original not only in Uglich, but in the whole of Russia, and was given the name 'Wonderful'.

The Rybinsk Reservoir was created in the early 1940s by the dam of the Rybinsk hydro-electric power station, built where the Volga turns almost 180 degrees from north to south-east. This reservoir, one of the world's largest man-made lakes (4,580 sq. km.), flooded not only part of the Volga valley, but also the lower reaches of its tributaries, the Sheksna and the Mologa. The creation of the Rybinsk Reservoir resulted in the inundation of 700 villages and the old town of Mologa, at the confluence of the Mologa River and the Volga, which had five churches and a convent dedicated to St Athanasius. Today all of this reposes under the surface of the artificial lake.

The Rybinsk Reservoir lies on the route of vessels cruising to the Russian North. They need several hours to cross it, after which they continue along the Sheksna, a part of the old trade route linking central Russia and the Volga with the North and the Baltic Sea. Here, at the

juncture of the Tver, Yaroslavl and Vologda regions, the population is very sparse: the only town of any size is Cherepovets, at the northern-most end of the Rybinsk Reservoir, where the Sheksna flows into it.

Cherepovets (580 km. by road from Moscow) was granted civic status in 1777, having been until then a settlement attached to the local Resurrection Monastery. Until the mid-20th century, it remained a small provincial town, but after the construction of a metallurgical plant, developed into the industrial centre of Vologda Region and the entire area, and now has over 300,000 inhabitants. The ethnography museum and the museum of Vassily Vereshchagin, an artist famous for his battle scenes, are worth visiting.

Along the Sheksna. On leaving Cherepovets, ships continue their north-bound voyage along the Sheksna River, one of the most beauti-ful in this part of Russia and the largest left-bank tributary of the Upper Volga. From olden times this river served as the route followed by Slavs

27. View of the Cyril-Belozero Monastery from Lake Siverskoe. The first monasteries in the Russian North were built along the banks of rivers or on the shores of lakes. Some became fortresses, and also served as outposts spreading the influence of the central authorities.

travelling north, extending the influence of the Russian state. The Sheksna has always been famous for its fish. In the 16th century the German Heinrich Staden, who served with Ivan the Terrible's special guard (the dreaded *Oprichniki*), wrote in his notes about Muscovy: 'Along the Sheksna River there are neither towns nor castles, but wooden piles are driven into the bottom of the river, and on these they catch sturgeon swimming up from the Caspian Sea to the White Lake. This sturgeon is consumed at the court of the Grand Duke.'

Though there were no 'towns or castles' along the Sheksna in olden times, there were many old settlements along its banks, most of them depopulated in the 18th and 19th centuries. The only one which expanded was the village of Sheksna, being on the railway line from St Petersburg to Vologda.

The Northern Dvina System. In the middle reaches of the river, the Sheksna is joined by another navigation route linking the Sheksna (the Volga basin) with the Sukhona (the Northern Dvina basin). This

28. The wall of the New Town with the Vologodskaya Tower. This massive, octagonal structure with its shallow roof, topped by a look-out post, is easily distinguished from the other towers of the Cyril-Belozero Monastery.

Northern Dvina System, as it is called, is one of the oldest artificial waterways in Russia. It was originally planned by Peter the Great, but its construction was completed only between 1825 and 1828. Previously named after a relation of Emperor Paul I, Duke Alexander of Wurttemberg, commander-in-chief of the department of communications and responsible for project designs, this navigation system includes Lake Kubenskoe, Lake Severskoe, and a number of canals. The total length of the Northern Dvina System, linking the Volga basin with the port of Arkhangelsk on the White Sea coast, is 133 kilometres. Following the construction of the railway line between Moscow and Arkhangelsk, its importance declined, but on the eve of the First World War it once again became the topic of animated debate. In 1909, a meeting of the Vologda land assembly examined an ambitious project to transform the Duke of Wurttemberg Canal into an integral part of a vast waterway network stretching from St Petersburg to Irkutsk, but this grandiose scheme was soon abandoned. After the construction of the White Sea-Baltic Sea Canal, the Northern Dvina System lost any importance, and now only small boats and tourist vessels pass though its wooden locks.

The true gems of this area are the few small old towns lying along the more northerly banks of the Sheksna such as the town of Kirillov with the nearby monasteries of Cyril-Belozero, Goritsi and Ferapont.

Leaving Uglich in the afternoon, tourist boats arrive at Goritsi quay the following morning, about two days after departure from Moscow. From here, a bus takes passengers the seven kilometres to Kirillov.

29. Part of the monastery's
defences: the Bolshaya
Merezhennaya or Belozerskaya
Tower, and the Kosaya Tower
(17th century). Having become
in the 17th century one of the
most strongly fortified monasteries in Russia, the Cyril-
Belozero Monastery never afterwards suffered enemy attack.

CYRIL AND FERAPONT

Goritsi. Close to the quay at Goritsi stands the Resurrection
Convent, founded in 1544 by Princess Yefrosinia, the wife of Prince
Andrei Staritsky, youngest son of Ivan III. In 1563 she and her son,
Prince Vladimir Staritsky, a cousin of the Tsar, were discovered to be
implicated in a plot, and Ivan IV, 'the Terrible', forced her to take the
veil and exiled her to the Resurrection Convent. Both in Staritsa, not
far from Tver, and at Goritsi, she ran workshops which produced
shrouds and cloths with Christ's image and altar cloths embroidered in
gold and silver. In 1569, after her son and his entire family had been
murdered by Ivan the Terrible, Yefrosinia was drowned in the Sheksna
on the Tsar's orders. Among the convent buildings which have survived
is the Resurrection Cathedral, built in 1544 by Yefrosinia, to which was
later added the small church of Dmitry, built prior to 1611 by Tsaritsa
Maria Nagaya in memory of her murdered son. The bell-tower erected
at the same time was completely reconstructed in the 18th century. The
remaining convent buildings—the Trinity Church, raised over the
graves of the nun Yevdokia (Yefrosinia) and her kinswoman Alexandra,
and the low wall—date from the first half of the 19th century.

Cyril-Belozero Monastery and Kirillov. The town of Kirillov,
lying on the shores of Lake Siverskoe and three smaller lakes, Dolgoe,
Lunskoe and Pokrovskoe, originated as a settlement near the monastery.

30. The Church of the Archangel Gabriel (1531-1534) was built with money donated to the monastery by Grand Duke Vassily III. Next to the church stands a bell-tower (1757-1761) and the Presentation Church (1519). Behind, to the right, is the Assumption Cathedral (1497), the oldest building in the monastery.

When it was granted civic status in 1775, an attempt was made to reconstruct it according to a regular plan, but this was never completed.

The town grew up around the ancient and majestic Cyril-Belozero Monastery, one of the largest in northern Russia, covering an area of around 12 hectares. In the 14th and 15th centuries there was a bitter conflict between Moscow and Novgorod for possession of these northern territories, named Belozerie after the biggest lake in the area, Beloe (White), and the monasteries built here served to consolidate the influence of the Muscovite princes.

The Cyril-Belozero Monastery, established in 1397, was named in honour of its founder, the monk Cyril from the Simonov Monastery in Moscow, a disciple of Sergius of Radonezh, founder of the St Sergius-Trinity Monastery in Sergiev Posad (Zagorsk) and one of the most honoured saints in the Russian Orthodox Church. Cyril came from the old boyar family of the Veliaminovs, who won renown in the battle of the Kulikovo Field in 1380. An archimandrite at the Simonov Monastery, he left Moscow for the North accompanied by another monk called Ferapont, who founded his own monastery a little later.

By the mid-15th century, the Cyril-Belozero Monastery was already well known in Russia, and its wealth and influence continued to grow. It also played a role in political affairs. In 1447, Vassily II, exiled to Uglich, made a pilgrimage to Kirillov, and Trifon, then father superior of the monastery, released him from his 'kiss of the cross', that is, freed him from his oath (sealed by kissing a cross) not to fight for the throne. That same year, Vassily the Dark took back the throne of

Moscow. Not unnaturally, he then did all he could to help the Cyril-Belozero Monastery.

Building in stone began at the monastery at the end of the 15th century: the Assumption Church (the monastery was originally called the Assumption Monastery) was erected in 1497 on the site of an earlier wooden church of the same name. In the 16th century, the scale of building was such that hired stonemasons proved insufficient, and the monastery began to train its own artisans. The Church of St John the Baptist, one of the many built at this time, was raised on a hill not far from the spot where Cyril had lived in his cell. Soon a cluster of auxiliary buildings appeared here, and the site became a separate monastery called Gorny (Upper) or Maly (Small) Ivanovsky.

Settlements of craftsmen sprang up around the monastery walls, in time becoming the nucleus of the town of Kirillov. The wooden ladles and drinking bowls with ornamental carving produced in quantity at Kirillov were in great demand throughout Russia. Attached to the monastery there were also smithies and leather workshops, while in the monastery itself icon painting flourished from the 15th century. The library held a very valuable collection of manuscripts and books. Between the 15th and the 17th centuries it was one of the largest libraries in Russia: according to information from the 17th century, it contained up to 1,900 volumes, some of them very old and rare. The greater part of this collection is now kept in the Russian Museum and the M.E. Saltykov-Shchedrin Library in St Petersburg.

The monastery continued to attract the attention of the grand dukes. Still childless after twenty years of marriage to Solomonia Saburova, Vassily III sent his wife to a convent in Suzdal and married Yelena Glinskaya. However, this union also failed to meet his hopes: he still had no heir. Then, in 1528, he set off on a pilgrimage to Belozero, and while at the Cyril Monastery prayed for a son. Two years later, the future Ivan the Terrible was born. In the 1560s, Ivan the Terrible himself visited the monastery and there made his confession, repenting his sins and intending to become a monk. In 1568 a special cell was even made ready for him, but he never relinquished his throne.

In the second half of the 16th century a wall was built first around the large Assumption Monastery, and then the Small Ivanovsky Monastery. This proved to be very opportune: with the 17th century came the Time of Troubles, and Russian towns in the North were plundered by the troops of the second false Dmitry, and then by Polish-Lithuanian invaders. Behind the monastery walls, the smiths made armour and cannon, preparing to repel the enemy. In August 1612, Polish-Lithuanian troops appeared at Kirillov and pillaged the settlements around the monastery. Rumours of the monastery's wealth had reached their ears, and in December they launched an attack against it from both land and water. Although defeated at the walls, the enemy troops inflicted enormous damage on the monastery.

Following the harsh lesson delivered by the Polish-Lithuanian invaders, in the 1660s the monks began the construction of a huge second wall which encompassed all the buildings and turned the monastery into an impregnable fortress. In the uneasy atmosphere of increasingly frequent peasant uprisings and revolts by the urban poor, the monastery also became a safe haven from popular discontent. Tsar Alexei Mikhailovich hastily sent his close friend and mentor, the boyar B.I. Morozov, to this monastery to save him from the fury of the insurgents. Having suppressed the rebellion and brought his favourite back to Moscow, the Tsar rewarded the monastery with the enormous sum of 45,000 rubles. To this Morozov then added a further 5,000. This

31. The Kotelnaya and Kuznechnaya towers of the Cyril-Belozero Monastery. Candles were made on the ground floor of the Kotelnaya Tower, and there are copper cauldrons (which account for its name) in the next chamber. The Kuznechnaya Tower got its name from the smithy which stood next to it.

32. The Transfiguration Church (1595) over the Water Gates, which was modelled on the Church of Johann Lestvichnik over the monastery's Holy Gates.

money was spent on raising new monastery walls and towers, a task that took some fifteen years to complete. However, these fortifications were never needed: thereafter, major military and political events bypassed this part of Russia.

In the 17th century, the Cyril-Belozero Monastery was named among the three richest in the country, alongside the St Sergius-Trinity Monastery and the Solovetsky Monastery. Nonetheless, the Belozero area was gradually becoming a provincial backwater.

From the second half of the 17th to the 19th century the Cyril-Belozero Monastery continued to play its role as a state prison. The most famous name among those exiled here in the 17th century was Patriarch Nikon, whose reforms led to a schism in the Russian Church.

In the 18th century, the district and local courts and the treasury were located in the so-called New Town fortress, and only the town council and the magistrate had their offices outside its walls. The monastery was closed in 1923, and the following year was turned into a museum and park.

The oldest building in the monastery is the Assumption Church, the third stone church to be built in the Russian North (the other two are at the Stone Saviour Monastery on Lake Kubenskoe, and at the Ferapont Monastery). The 'Great Church', as one chronicler called it, was built in 1497 in just five months by 20 Rostov craftsmen under Prokhor of Rostov. The Assumption Church we can see today has been rebuilt, and the many additions have altered its originally austere appearance. The small Vladimir Church, adjoining its northern wall,

33. The Svitochnaya Tower, on a headland jutting into Lake Siverskoe on the southern side of the monastery, is one of the finest surviving towers of the Old Town (16th century). Here, on the ground floor, lived the monastery servants who did the washing. Hence the name of the tower: 'svitki' (cassocks).

was raised over the grave of Prince Vorotinsky in 1554 and later served as the mausoleum of the Vorotinsky family. Like the Assumption Church, this also has a band of decorative brickwork running around the walls and the drum of the dome. The composition of the Assumption Church became even more complex in 1645, when the Epiphany Church was added to the northern wall of the Vladimir Church, over the grave of Prince Teliatevsky. Finally, adjoining the southern wall of the Assumption Church is the Cyril Church (1792-1794), built to replace the earlier 16th-century church raised over the founder's grave.

The interior of the Assumption Church was decorated in 1641 by painters from a workshop under the Kostroma artist Liubim Ageev, a well-known master of the first half of the 17th century: his name is mentioned among those who painted the frescoes in the Assumption Cathedral in Moscow. The enormous iconostasis, like the church itself, has undergone repeated modifications. The royal gates in their silver frame were a gift from Tsar Alexei Mikhailovich in 1645.

The main entrance to the Great Assumption Monastery was through the Holy Gates, above which the Church of Johann Lestvichnik was built. The gates and church are part of the original 16th-century monastery wall. The Holy Gates, dating from 1532, have two arched passageways, a style typical of monastic architecture at that period. Though most of the painting which once adorned them has disappeared, the image of Sabaoth and also of the Virgin Mary with Moscow Metropolitans (1585) can still be discerned.

The Church of Johann Lestvichnik was built over the gates between 1569 and 1572 with money donated by the tsareviches Johann and Fedor, sons of Ivan the Terrible. The church once had two domes, the second above the south-eastern chapel, a feature characteristic of church architecture in the Vologda countryside.

A monumental treasury adjoins the Holy Gates on the western side, forming one line with the wall. The ground floor, built in the mid-16th century, was used as an office, while the first floor, from the second half of the 17th century, was used to store all kinds of supplies. The mica windows and brick floor have survived, enabling us to gain some impression of the interior of 17th-century store-rooms.

To the east and south-west of the Church of Johann Lestvichnik there is an entire complex of monks' cells. The father superior's chambers, the monastery's archives and a part of the monastic building were erected in 1647/1648. In the late 17th and early 18th centuries, priests' cells were built, and a second storey added to the entire complex.

Alongside the southern chapel of the Assumption Cathedral stands the Church of Archangel Gabriel, built between 1531 and 1534 with money donated by Grand Duke Vassily III. A striking feature of the whole ensemble is the bell-tower (1757-1761), the tallest building in the monastery, which echoes the vertical lines of the corner towers.

In 1519, shortly after completion of the Assumption Cathedral, the refectory and Presentation Church were built. In size, the refectory of the Cyril-Belozero Monastery is one of the largest of its day, indicating the number of monks who gathered there for meals. Adjoining it, to the south is the cellarer's house (mid-17th century) with decorated window frames. On the ground floor are the monks' cells, and on the first floor, store-rooms. Adjoining the refectory on the west side are the kitchen (16th century) and the bakery, built in the 1680s near the monastery walls. As few such auxiliary buildings have survived, these are of particular value.

The Water Gates (16th century), which have both a large and a small passageway, lead out of the monastery towards Lake Siverskoe. In 1595 the Transfiguration Church was built over these gates, its design echoing the lines of the Church of Johann Lestvichnik over the Holy Gates. Inside the church there is an iconostasis with icons dating from the end of the 16th century, the work of local artists.

The living quarters and auxiliary buildings, together with the infirmary buildings, form a small complex in the south-eastern corner of the monastery, They were built in the 1640s, a period of revival in construction following the end of the Time of Troubles. The Large Infirmary (1643-1644), as tradition required, had a church built next to it. This is the Church of Euphimius (1646), which differs from the other monastery buildings in having a hip roof, but like the other churches is decorated with ornamental brickwork. Another unusual feature is the small belfry of a type found on a number of churches in Pskov and Novgorod.

The main building in the Maly (or Gorny) Ivanovsky Monastery is the Church of St John the Baptist, erected between 1531 and 1534, together with the Church of the Archangel Gabriel, with money donated by Grand Duke Vassily III. It is probable that both were built by the same team of craftsmen. The church has an iconostasis dating from the 18th century with icons in the baroque style.

It is thought that it was on this same hill where the Church of St John the Baptist now stands that the monastery was originally founded. On the northern slope, where Cyril and Ferapont had their first earthen shelter, stands a wooden cross with a stone canopy. The wooden chapel

42

36. Monks in Russia always chose the most beautiful site in the area to build a monastery, and the monastery or church is always the dominant feature and main embellishment of the local landscape.

here, which, according to tradition, was built by Cyril himself, is undoubtedly very old: this type of structure was widespread in the Russian North in the 14th and 15th centuries. Inside, there is a severely scarred wooden cross which was believed to cure toothache.

On the opposite slope, next to the church of St John the Baptist, is the refectory and the Church of St Sergius of Radonezh, built in 1560, shortly after the small monastery had finally separated from the Cyril-Belozero Monastery. Tradition has it that the money was donated by Ivan the Terrible. Over the church is a belfry with arched apertures—a rare feature in churches of this kind, and apparently copied from older buildings in the nearby Ferapont and Stone Saviour monasteries. Further to the east, by the monastery wall, is the Small Infirmary, built in the 1730s. Curiously, this building has little in common with the architecture of the 18th century, but follows the traditions of the 16th and 17th centuries.

On the territory of the New Town, that is, the area between the old and new monastery walls, the wooden Deposition Church, brought from the village of Borodava, stands in a small inner courtyard. This modest building, raised in 1486 with money donated by Ioasaf, Archbishop of Rostov, is older than all the famous stone buildings of the North. Such small, simple, wooden churches usually sprang up in the North with the founding of new monasteries. Some valuable 16th-century icons from this church are now in the Andrei Rublev Museum of Old Russian Art in Moscow. The windmill nearby, brought from the village of Gorky, was built in the last century.

37. In comparison with the Cyril-Belozero Monastery, the Ferapont Monastery seems very small and intimate. The stone wall which now surrounds it was built only in the last century to replace a wooden fence. The main monastery entrance was through the traditionally named Holy Gates. Above these stand the Epiphany Church and the Ferapont Church (1649).

The monastery fortifications are of great interest from both the architectural and the military point of view. Construction work on the original (inner) wall—the Old Town—continued throughout the whole of the 16th century. Its total length is 1,000 metres, its maximum height about 5.2 metres, and its width 1.5 metres.

Begun after the Polish-Swedish invasion, construction of the New Town—an even more massive series of walls—lasted from 1654 to 1680 and extended the territory of the monastery from six to 12 hectares. The new wall was 732 metres long, around 10 metres high, and seven metres wide. By the end of the 17th century, the Cyril-Belozero Monastery had become one of the most impregnable fortresses in Russia. The towers and high walls are arranged in three levels. As the monastery did not have to repel any further armed incursions, the lowest, closed level was transformed into living quarters.

The rectangular towers, Kazanskaya and Kosaya, are located in the centre of the walls, while at the four corners are the more impressive polygonal towers: Kuznechnaya, Vologodskaya, Moskovskaya and Belozerskaya (also known as Bolshaya Merezhennaya). The sixteen-sided Kuznechnaya, Moskovskaya and Belozerskaya towers are particularly awesome with their smooth walls pierced only by narrow loopholes. The gate towers are lower. In the Kosaya Tower the passageway is quite unusual, extending at an angle rather than leading straight through, which explains the name of the tower (*kosaya* means 'slanting'). The Kazanskaya Tower, the main entrance to the monastery, has massive gates made of large, iron-bound beams.

38. The Cathedral of the Nativity of the Virgin (1490), the oldest building in the Ferapont Monastery, the bell-tower (17th century), and the Annunciation Church (1530-1534). All three buildings were linked in the 17th century by covered, two-level passages. These original wooden passages 'which were dangerous to walk through' were demolished and replaced by new ones in 1797.

The Kirillov Museum of History and Art, located inside the monastery, houses valuable examples of medieval icon painting, embroidery, applied and traditional art. One of the oldest items, dating from the early 15th century, is the Assumption icon thought to be the work of the artist Dyonisius Glushitsky (not to be confused with the renowned medieval Russian icon painter Dyonisius, who painted the frescoes in the Ferapont Monastery). He also painted the image of Cyril himself, possibly during the latter's own lifetime. The pride of the museum is the wonderful collection of icons, dating from 1496 and 1497, which come from the iconostasis of the Assumption Cathedral. Sixty icons have survived, half of which are displayed here and the remainder in museums in Moscow and St Petersburg. The museum also includes works by Dyonisius (of Ferapontovo) and his pupils.

Ferapont Monastery stands on a hill between lakes Borodavskoe and Paskoe (20 km. from Kirillov, 115 km. from Vologda). Huge trees surround the monastery, so that, as one approaches, only the domes of

48

39. The Annunciation Church,
the second stone building in the
Ferapont Monastery, was raised
with money donated by Grand
Duke Vassily III, to whom a
long-awaited heir, the future
Tsar Ivan the Terrible, was
born after his visit here. The
bell-tower has retained its original appearance.

40. Ferapont is famous above all for the frescoes in the Nativity Cathedral, painted by one of the most renowned artists of medieval Russia, Dyonisius (1440-1503). The church with its frescoes is open for private visitors from May to September during ventilation hours (a special micro-climate is maintained in the church to protect the frescoes).

41. Fresco by Dyonisius on the west portal of the Nativity Cathedral. The tradition of decorating the exterior of churches, in particular the main, western façade, has its roots in the distant past, and very few such works have survived. Fortunately, from the 17th century on a covered passage extended from this façade to the bell-tower and so protected the painting.

its churches can be seen, rising proudly above the tree-tops.

The monastery was founded in 1398 by Ferapont, who came from the boyar family of Poskochin. He took his vows at the Simonov Monastery in Moscow and came to the North together with Cyril. However, he did not stay long with Cyril at Lake Siverskoe but founded his own monastery. The 14th and 15th centuries were the heyday of monastery building in Russia: 150 were founded between 1340 and 1440. Like Cyril, Ferapont was soon joined by a growing number of monks, who built themselves cells and in 1409 erected a wooden church dedicated to the Nativity of the Virgin, followed by a refectory. Ten years later the name of this new monastery reached the ears of Prince Andrei Dmitrievich, who sent for Ferapont to come to him at Mozhaisk, where he founded the Luzhetsky Monastery and died in 1426.

The subsequent development of the Ferapont Monastery is linked to the name of Father Superior Martinian, a prominent church figure of the 15th century, who had earlier been a monk at the Cyril Monastery and a disciple of Cyril. Under his leadership, the Ferapont Monastery flourished, becoming a major spiritual and educational centre by the end of the century. Having spent twelve years at Ferapontovo, Martinian left for the St Sergius-Trinity Monastery, where he succeeded Sergius of Radonezh. In his old age Martinian returned to Ferapontovo, where he died in 1483.

Archbishop Ioasaf of Rostov, a figure no less renowned in the Russian Church, also spent many years at Ferapont. A descendant of Rurik and a close relative of Grand Duke Ivan III, he belonged to the

42. Fresco by Dyonisius glorifying the Mother of God (Virgin Mary) in the northern lunette of the Nativity Cathedral. The Soviet artist N.M. Chernishev once put forward the interesting suggestion that Dyonisius had made his paints by grinding multi-coloured pebbles from the shores of Lake Borodavskoe, which artists have shown to be possible. However, recent research has shown that Dyonisius actually used pigments brought in specially for the purpose.

43. Lake Borodavskoe (overleaf). During his exile at Ferapont from 1666 to 1676, Patriarch Nikon had a cruciform island created in the lake, on which he raised a wooden cross, where he spent long hours in prayer.

44. Like the first monks of the Christian era who sought solitude in deserts and mountains, so hermits in Russia left for the remote regions and virgin forests of the North. The harsh beauty of the northern landscape, with its brief, sultry summer and long, cold winter served, as it were, to intensify their contemplation of the world. (pp. 56-57)

wealthy and aristocratic Obolensky family: his secular name was Prince Ivan Nikitich. Renouncing his wealth and rank, he took vows as the monk Ioasaf at the Ferapont Monastery. Soon he rose in the church hierarchy, becoming the head of one of the most illustrious and ancient Russian dioceses. In 1488 Ioasaf suddenly left Rostov and returned to the remote northern monastery in which he had taken his vows. It is possible that a dispute with Grand Duke Ivan III may have caused him to be exiled there.

Whatever the case may be, the beginning of stone construction at the monastery is linked to the name of Ioasaf. His return here in 1488, after eight years at the head of the Rostov diocese, coincided with a large fire in which many of its buildings were reduced to ashes. Luckily, a 'treasure' kept in the former archbishop's cell and intended to meet the needs of the monastery survived the conflagration.

The Cathedral of the Nativity of the Virgin was obviously resurrected out of the ruins using this 'treasure'. It is also possible that it was Ioasaf who invited Dyonisius to paint the frescoes in the new cathedral, either because he himself knew the artist's work or because he had heard of the artist from a relative, Vassian Rylo, Archbishop of Rostov, who commissioned the icons for the Assumption Cathedral in Moscow, also painted by Dyonisius.

Ioasaf spent about twenty-five years at the Ferapont Monastery, passing the last of them in total silence. He died in 1513 and was buried at the feet of his mentor, Martinian, who had received his vows as a monk. Today we remember him thanks to the wooden church from the village of Borodava, now at the Cyril-Belozero Monastery, the Nativity Cathedral in Ferapontovo, with its frescoes by Dyonisius, and almost all the icons painted during his time at the monastery, most of which, however, are no longer at Ferapontovo, but are part of collections in Moscow, St Petersburg and Kirillov.

The Ferapont Monastery played a significant role in the development of this remote area. In the reign of Ivan the Terrible, it was granted a number of benefits and privileges: in addition to farmland, it also had the right to fish in a number of places. During the 16th and 17th centuries, several buildings were added, but, unlike the Cyril Monastery, it never became a fortress; it had a wooden fence around it until the 19th century. Indeed, because of this lack of defences, the monastery was sacked in 1614 by marauding Polish troops.

Because of its isolated position, Ferapont, like the neighbouring monasteries, became a place of exile. Patriarch Nikon was confined here from 1666 to 1676. Though deposed by a church council, he had many supporters and was therefore conveyed to his place of exile with a speed unusual for those days: the journey from Moscow, a distance of 600 kilometres, was completed in six days! To begin with, Nikon was kept in complete isolation, with iron bars on his windows. He arrived accompanied by a special police officer and 20 soldiers to guard the only prisoner at the monastery.

Nikon, however, continued to hope for a speedy return—all the more so as rumours of plans to release him reached him from Moscow—and he began to demand that those around him pay him due respect as the patriarch. The monastery authorities, who could not know whether or not the former patriarch's disgrace would prove permanent, decided to heed his orders. In 1667 work began to build a new cell for him, and the Epiphany Church was placed at his disposal. By orders of the Tsar, he was also granted fishing rights in Lake Borodavskoe. Nikon then ordered the creation of a stone island in the shape of a cross in middle of the lake, where he set up a wooden cross

and spent long periods in prayer. The wooden cross stood on the island until 1676, when it was removed on the orders of Patriarch Ioakim.

The election in 1674 of Ioakim, an old enemy of Nikon, as patriarch led to harsher conditions of exile at the monastery. Following the death of Tsar Alexei Mikhailovich in 1676, Nikon's position deteriorated sharply. Ioakim levelled numerous accusations against him, both ridiculous and also serious. He was charged, for example, with having contacts with messengers sent by Stepan Razin, who led an uprising which lasted several years and spread over a large area of the country, becoming in effect a peasant war against the boyars. This charge was sufficient for Nikon to be transferred to the Cyril-Belozero Monastery and placed under strict surveillance. It was not until 1681 that Nikon, now old and sick, was permitted to return to the New Jerusalem Monastery of the Resurrection which he himself had founded outside Moscow, but he never arrived there, dying on the way at Yaroslavl.

The ten years which Nikon spent at Ferapontovo were the last notable episode in the history of the monastery, which gradually became impoverished and fell into disrepair. The hardest period came in the 18th century, particularly during the reign of Catherine II. In 1764, hundreds of monasteries around the country were closed, leaving only 385 out of the previous 681. In 1798, the Ferapont Monastery was also closed, and its churches became parish churches. In 1857 the dilapidated wooden fence was replaced with a stone wall, parts of which have survived.

For a while, however, the monastery enjoyed a new lease of life in connection with its 500th anniversary, when a convent was opened here through the efforts of Taisia, a member of the aristocratic Soloviev family, who served as mother superior. With the help of a few nuns who moved with her from the Leushinsky Convent, Taisia began to restore the abandoned and dilapidated monastery buildings. She succeeded in winning the support of many well-known historians and archaeologists, who then supervised the restoration work. Taisia died in 1915, and was buried in her beloved Leushinsky Convent. The tomb of the famous mother superior of Ferapontovo now lies at the bottom of the Rybinsk Reservoir.

The restoration of the monastery begun by Taisia stopped in 1917. In 1922, when church valuables were being confiscated all around the country, the Ferapont and Cyril monasteries were also affected. The silver shrine of St Cyril, donated in the 17th century by the Sheremetev family, was removed, together with church vessels, a lamp donated by Nicholas II, and the precious metal mounts of old icons. Then the monastery was subjected to impossible taxes, and in 1925 all its land, cattle and implements were handed over to the local state farm. It was only later that the monastery was converted into a museum, called the Museum of Dyonisius Frescoes.

In the 1940s the village of Ferapontovo comprised only a dozen houses. Today that number has increased slightly thanks to the fame of the frescoes and to the fact that, since the opening up of tourist itineraries along the Volga-Baltic Canal in the 1960s, the monastery has become one of the chief sights of the area. A macadam road now runs directly to the village, and a hotel has been built.

The main entrance to the monastery was through a stone gateway in the western wall bearing the traditional name of Holy Gates. Over this entrance are two small churches, the Epiphany Church and the Ferapont Church, constructed in 1649.

The oldest building in the monastery, the Cathedral of the Nativity of the Virgin (1490), was only the second stone church to be built in

45. The Assumption Church (1552-1553), the oldest in Belozersk, was built by the Rostov architects Goriain Grigoriev Tsarev and Tretiak Borisov Rostovka with money donated by parishioners.

46. The Epiphany Church (mid-18th century) in Belozersk. The design of this small winter (heated) church is typical of the provincial architecture of the day.

47, 48. The Church of Elijah the Prophet (1690-1696), the only surviving wooden church in Belozersk. Because of the abundance of building timber and the carpentry skills of local craftsmen, the tradition of wooden architecture in the North continued for centuries after stone churches had begun to be built elsewhere.

49. Although the ramparts of Belozersk have become considerably reduced in height, they are still impressive, reaching up to 20 metres. On the left is the Transfiguration Cathedral (1668-1670).

the Russian North. It was probably the work of Rostov craftsmen, as was the church at the Stone Saviour Monastery before it, and the stone church in the Cyril Monastery later. After the cathedral had been completed, it was surrounded by a covered gallery on three sides. An original feature of this is the small church built in the north-western section and representing both a church and a belfry in one. In addition to the traditional decorative elements, the cathedral also has a band of ornamental tiles depicting lilies and snow leopards.

Above all, however, the Ferapont Monastery is famous for its cathedral frescoes, masterpieces of medieval Russian art, by Dyonisius, who also painted icons for the iconostasis. The life of Dyonisius, the most renowned artist of his age, was one of rare good fortune. From his early years he enjoyed the advantage of having highly placed patrons, and was able to work in the most prestigious cathedrals and monasteries. His work in the Assumption Cathedral in the Moscow Kremlin won high praise from his contemporaries.

There is no earlier monumental painting in Russia which has survived, as have the frescoes at Ferapontovo, almost unchanged. According to the inscription left by Dyonisius over the northern portal of the church—itself a rarity for medieval Russia—the artist and his sons, Theodosius and Vladimir, painted the entire cathedral during the two summer seasons of 1502 and 1503.

The Nativity Cathedral frescoes are the last major work of Dyonisius. By 1508, when the frescoes in the Annunciation Cathedral in the Moscow Kremlin were painted by artists from a workshop under

his son Theodosius, Dyonisius himself had either died or retired.

The Ferapontovo frescoes were forgotten for many years. They were recalled only at the turn of this century when I.I. Brilliantov, the son of the priest from the neighbouring village of Tsipino, published his monograph on Ferapontovo. He was the first to mention the signature of Dyonisius and his sons, and advance the suggestion that this was the same artist who, in 1481, together with two other icon painters, had been invited to paint the icons for the iconostasis in the Assumption Cathedral in the Moscow Kremlin.

The second-oldest stone building in the monastery is the Annunciation Church, erected between 1530 and 1534 with money donated by Grand Duke Vassily III. Following his visit to the

51. Belozersk is one of the oldest Russian towns. According to the earliest extant chronicle, 'The Tale of Bygone Years' by Nestor, in the 9th century Belozersk was ruled by Sineus, brother of Rurik, founder of the first dynasty of Russian rulers, which lasted for over seven centuries.

monastery, the long-awaited heir, the future Ivan the Terrible, was born, and to mark this joyous event Vassily ordered the construction of this church, and also the churches of Archangel Gabriel and St John the Baptist in the Cyril-Belozero Monastery. Inside the Annunciation Church, in the upper level, there is a row of small chambers that formerly served as a secret repository and book-store. Interestingly, up above these, in the previously open embrasures of the arches, bells were hung, indicating that this church belonged to the unusual type which combined both a church and a belfry in one. Now the church and refectory house a museum with copies of the frescoes by Dyonisius made by N.V. Gusev.

The Nativity Cathedral and the Annunciation Church are linked by covered passageways dating from the end of the 18th century. In the centre, a 17th-century, three-tiered bell-tower rises above them.

The Martinian Church (1641), adjoining the southern wall of the Nativity Cathedral, was raised over the tomb of Father Superior Martinian, who was canonised in the 16th century. The wooden shrine of Martinian (17th century) can still be seen inside the church. On the northern wall there are fragments of paintings thought to be the work of one of Dyonisius's assistants.

Adjoining the Holy Gates to the south is the Treasury Chamber, constructed in the mid-16th century.

To the south of the monastery rises the highest hill in the area, Tsipina Gora, covered in greenery, which has long been a favourite place for folk dancing and celebrations. At its foot, beside the small, peaceful Lake Ilyinskoe, there is an interesting example of wooden architecture: the Church of Elijah the Prophet in Tsipino Cemetery (1755). The village of Tsipino, which belonged to the Ferapont Monastery, is mentioned as early as the beginning of the 16th century. In the 19th century, the parish of this church covered about twenty small villages and had more than a thousand parishioners. Half of these villages no longer exist.

Belozersk and the White Lake. The Sheksna River, along which the ship continues its route from Goritsi to the north, towards the Land of the White Nights, has its source in the large, almost circular Lake Beloe (area: 1,120 sq. km.; diametre: about 40 km.). The shallowness of the lake, only four to five metres deep, accounts for the whitish-grey colour of its surface that probably explains its name, White Lake. Its waters, which warm quickly in summer, abound in fish.

Not far from the spot where the Sheksna flows out of the lake stands the town of Belozersk, one of the oldest in Russia, and probably the only one to change its location twice in its history. When first mentioned in chronicles in 862 as Belozero (the name of the town up to the reign of Catherine II), it was located on the northern shore of the lake, next to the village of Kisnema, which stands there today. Originally the town was settled by the Ves, probably the ancestors of the present-day Veps. The exact date of the founding of the town is not known, but in 862, when Rurik, Sineus and Truvor were invited to govern Russia (the beginning of the Rurik dynasty, which ruled first Kievan Rus and then the entire state of Muscovy), the place was already important enough to be chosen as the residence of the second of the three brothers.

Later, in the 10th century, on the orders of Prince Vladimir of Kiev, the town was moved to the opposite, southern shore, at the point where the Sheksna flows out of the lake and the small village of Krokhino now stands.

The princes of Kiev ruled over Belozero up to the death of Yaroslav the Wise, who, by tradition, built the first church in the town, dedicated to St Basil. Following his death in 1054, Belozero, together with Rostov, Pereslavl and Suzdal, became the patrimony of his son Vsevolod, and until the first third of the 13th century were part of the Rostov-Suzdal principality on the northern fringe of Russian territory.

Thanks to its remote location, the town escaped pillage by the Tatars in 1238, and it was here that Cyril, Bishop of Rostov, took refuge. When Prince Vasilko of Rostov died in battle fighting the Tatars, his son Gleb, who inherited Belozero, broke away from Rostov and established an independent principality whose territory covered the entire basin of Lake Beloe, the Sheksna and Lake Kubenskoe. At this

time people moved to Belozero from the central regions of Russia, which had suffered depredation. Though natural barriers hampered the northward advance of the Tatar troops, Prince Gleb Vasilkovich, taking no chances, ordered the raising of earthen ramparts for the town's defence. It was during his reign that several monasteries were founded around the town. He died in 1278, having become Prince of Rostov, and is buried in Rostov Veliki.

The principality of Belozero, ruled by Gleb's descendants, retained its independence until the early 1380s, when the town came under the rule of Grand Duke Dmitry Donskoi of Moscow. In 1389, Dmitry transferred this northern territory to his son Andrei, Prince of Mozhaisk. Belozero remained under the rule of the princes of Mozhaisk until 1485, when the town finally became part of the Muscovite principality.

However, the town stood at the source of the Sheksna only until 1352, when the plague wiped out most of the population. In 1363 and 1364, it was moved for a second time—on this occasion 17 kilometres to the west, where it stands today. The last reference to the 'old town of Belozero' was in 1398, when it was burnt by Novgorodian troops.

With the construction of the Cherepovets hydro-electric power station, the level of the Sheksna River rose by 11 metres, and most of the site of the old town is now under water. Excavations carried out urgently prior to the flooding revealed traces of old buildings, such as log cabins dating from the 9th to the 12th centuries, and other valuable finds.

Having moved to its new location at the junction of major trade routes, the town rapidly expanded and prospered. The economy of this area was based on crafts and trade, since the land was not very suitable for farming. The Belozero area and its centre, Belozero, now reached the high point of their development. Representatives of the large monasteries in Moscow and on the Upper Volga, and of the St Cyril Monastery, came here to trade, as did merchants from Tver and Novgorod. However, under Ivan III, the Belozero principality ceased to exist, and became simply the Belozero district. At the same time, at the end of the 15th century, on Ivan's orders the new town was surrounded by a massive rampart one kilometre long, and a wooden fortress with eight towers was erected.

The Polish invasion of 1612, which left the town devastated, and the shift of trade routes to the Baltic in the 18th century were blows from which Belozero never fully recovered. Nonetheless, from the 17th to the 19th centuries a number of stone churches, houses and administrative buildings were erected. 'A small town very rich in churches,' wrote a visitor to Belozersk at the very beginning of this century. There were ten monasteries around the town. When Russia's administrative boundaries were redrawn in 1777, the town of Belozero was officially renamed Belozersk.

The construction in the 1840s of a bypass canal enabling small ships to avoid the stormy waters of Lake Beloe gave the town a new lease of life. If there was a fair wind, ships crossed the lake quickly and easily, but if the wind changed suddenly or a storm arose, then the canal was safer and more convenient. As one witness noted in 1847, '1,500 vessels wintered on the canal and in the harbour'.

It was at Belozersk that sessions of the so-called ship tribunal were held to resolve disputes, mainly over pay, between ship-owners and the barge-haulage teams who pulled the boats upstream against the current, and along the canals. This upsurge in prosperity connected with increased shipping did not, however, last very long. At the beginning of the 20th century there were plans to build a railway line to

56. The modernisation of the Mariinsky navigation system in the 1950s and 1960s made it navigable for even the largest vessels of the river-sea class.

57. Lock No. 1 on the watershed between Lakes Beloe and Onega. Previously there were more than 20 small wooden locks between the Kovzha and the Vytegra. Today, just six locks form a huge 80-metre 'stairway' for shipping.

Belozersk, but the outbreak of the First World War in 1914 interrupted them and then they were forgotten.

Today Belozersk is a district centre of Vologda Region, a quiet, provincial town with a population of 13,000. Its position on the shores of Lake Beloe and on the banks of the bypass canal lends it a particular charm. One of the main sights of the town is the massive earthen ramparts, raised in 1487, after the town had finally come under the rule of Muscovy, when it was planned to make Belozersk a key fortress on the country's northern borders. The ramparts, which are up to 30 metres high, were surmounted by wooden walls and towers and surrounded by a moat. Some people believe that the ramparts predate the reign of Ivan III, and that at the end of the 15th century, when the moat was dug, the

58. Villages around Vytegra (overleaf), as elsewhere in the Russian North, are built along river banks. Rivers here often have rocky beds unsuitable for driving in piles, so wooden bridges rest on big log cribs placed along the current and packed with large boulders.

earth was simply used to increase the height of the existing ramparts. In 1758, the dilapidated wooden fortress was dismantled.

As in other Russian towns, this fortified section of Belozersk was called the Kremlin. It can be entered across the 18th-century arch-shaped bridge over the moat. In the centre of the Kremlin rises the majestic Transfiguration Cathedral (1668-1670), built on the orders of Tsar Fedor Alekseevich. Although the design of the church is typical for the period, individual details recall the architecture of the previous century. The ornamental geometric pattern and the broad portals, in particular, are clearly reminiscent of older monuments. The cathedral still contains a magnificent iconostasis from the 18th century executed in the baroque style, lavishly decorated with carving and sculptures.

59. Vytegra: detail of ornamental carving on a wooden chapel (1881) moved to the town from its original site on Besednaya (Conversation) Hill. It is believed to have got its name from the fact that Peter the Great conversed there with some of the townspeople while inspecting the site where he intended to have the canal built.

To the east of the cathedral is the Town Hall in the classical style prevalent in the first third of the 19th century. Also from this period is the Trading Rows (1840), a type of structure widespread in the provinces, comprising rows of shops on either side of the market square. In Belosersk only the southern row, five buildings with an arcade, has survived, the rectangular buildings with their attractively shaped arches together forming a single architectural ensemble.

The oldest building in Belozersk is the Assumption Church (1552-1553), erected on the orders of Ivan the Terrible. It is located outside the Kremlin, in the trade settlement, on the town's highest point. Though the Rostov craftsmen who built it took the Assumption Cathedral in the Cyril-Belozero Monastery as their model, it is not a

60. The Vologda area has always been noted for its dairy cattle and excellent milk products. Today Vologda butter is sold in Moscow's best shops and is one of the few export commodities of the country's food industry.

mere copy of its prototype, but resembles Novgorodian structures of the 16th century, which probably served as the standard for the Rostov builders. This resemblance to the architecture of Novgorod and Pskov is further accentuated by a certain unevenness in the plastered walls. The church has an 18th-century baroque iconostasis with a row of icons dating from the 16th century.

Not far from the Assumption Church is the small Epiphany Church, built in the baroque style in the mid-18th century.

One of the main sights of the town is to be found to the west of the Kremlin. This is the small, wooden Church of Elijah the Prophet (1690-1696), of the type described as multi-level: it is composed of two rectangular log structures set one on top the other and surmounted

61. Smaller vessels formerly took great risks venturing into Lake Onega, where violent storms were not uncommon. To ensure their safety, a bypass canal was built between the Vytegra estuary and the source of the Svir.

by an octahedron. Adjoining the church on the west is a refectory. Wooden churches, once so numerous in the Russian North and still to be found in Karelia and Arkhangelsk Region, are today very rare in Vologda Region.

The Church of the All-Merciful Saviour, which stands not far from the wharf, is notable for its originality and its tile ornamentation. It was built between 1716 and 1723, but, like many provincial structures, its design adheres to the architectural forms of the previous century. Its hip-roofed belfry is one of the town's landmarks.

A whole row of one-storey buildings, distinguished by contrasting red walls and white details, stretches along the canal to the north of the church. All these buildings date from 1846, as does the obelisk on the opposite bank of the canal, erected to mark its opening to shipping.

Also worth mentioning is the Church of St John the Baptist, built in 1810 in the classical style, which is not always included in guidebooks on Belozersk or shown to tourists. This is a pity, since recent research indicates that it was probably designed by the famous Russian architect, V.I. Bazhenov. An album discovered in the A. Shchusev Museum of Russian Architecture in Moscow contained sketches by Bazhenov for an unknown building, of which the general view, façade and cross-section proved to be identical to those of the Church of St John the Baptist in Belozersk. True, it is still not known why these sketches were put to use only ten years after the death of the architect, and in such a remote, provincial town as Belozersk.

Buildings in the classical style, dating from the first half and mid-

62. Because of the limited throughput of the old Mariinsky system, two-thirds of the vessels arriving in St Petersburg from Rybinsk were unable to get back before the end of the navigation season. This prompted the introduction of 'disposable' boats, mariinkas, which were used only once, to carry the cargo to St Petersburg, and afterwards were sold there as firewood.

63. Kizhi Island: the Chapel of the Three High Priests (17th-18th century), transferred here from the village of Kavgora in 1961. It was first placed on the island's southern tip, where it was overshadowed by the main Kizhi ensemble, and now graces the northern end of the island (overleaf).

dle of the last century, are well preserved in Belozersk and contribute to the overall character of the town. As a rule, they belonged to local merchants and high-ranking officials.

Belozersk was unaffected by Soviet industrialisation, and was thus able to preserve much of its former appearance and charm. Although some of the old churches and houses were destroyed or have now fallen into disrepair, the town has a neat appearance and does not create the impression of neglect. On the contrary, here one can feel the spirit of the Russian provinces.

Perhaps some people will also be struck by the beauty of the local women. They will not be the first: many visitors have admired their delicate, gentle features, and it is said that even Tsar Ivan the Terrible, on a visit to the town, remarked: 'What fine women you have!'

The voyage into the heartland of the White Nights country now continues from Lake Beloe along the Kovzha River, which flows into the lake from the north-west, the Vytegra River, and then the Volga-Baltic Canal, which joins the upper reaches of the two rivers. The watershed between the Kovzha and the Vytegra, linked by the canal, was the site of enormous construction work in the 1950s and 1960s, and is now a large system of complex engineering structures. However, the places located between Lake Beloe and Lake Onega, along the route of the Volga-Baltic Canal which runs through the area, are still remote backwaters, and even today not every village can be reached by road—a boat remains the most convenient form of transport.

SAILING TO KIZHI

Vytegra. The chain of locks ends at the town of Vytegra that straddles the river of the same name. In summer the town can be reached from Petrozavodsk by a three-hour trip by hydrofoil.

Antiquity is not something Vytegra can boast of. Very early in the 18th century, Peter the Great ordered a landing place to be built there. The Vianga landing, with warehouses and granaries lining the quay, served as a transhipment point for goods heading for St Petersburg from the Volga. However, the construction of the Vyshny Volochok Canal put paid to the goods traffic at the Vianga landing, and by 1773 the local population totalled a mere 21 souls.

The Vianga landing was given a new lease of life after a decree was issued in 1773 that a town be founded in the locality and named Vytegra after the river. The idea was to boost trade between St Petersburg and the country's central areas on the Volga and its tributaries. According to the urban plan approved in 1776, the streets were to be laid out on the grid system, a fairly common feature of the numerous reconstruction schemes for Russian cities at the time. There were also plans for a new administration centre and marketplace, and a bridge across the river, all in stone. However, the construction work took far longer than originally intended and few stone buildings were erected until the early decades of the 19th century. Before that, the local people stubbornly persisted in the old, familiar building techniques and made their houses of wood instead of following the 'model designs' they had been supplied with.

Once the Mariinsky waterway system was completed, navigation played an increasingly important role in the life of the town, and local trade and industry were considerably buoyed up. The town's coat of arms, appropriately, had a galliot stern in a golden field with the Russian merchant flag flying (the galliot was the chief type of merchantman at the time).

But, contrary to expectations, Vytegra never made it in the 19th century to the rank of main city of Olonets Province. The limited throughput capacity of the old Mariinsky system checked its further expansion and it remained a small provincial town at the back of beyond. By the 1830s, the use of stone in construction had virtually ceased, and the town, mostly built of wood, was a frequent victim of devastating fires. Only the building of the imposing Purification Cathedral in the early 1870s finally did something to improve its general aspect. Trade started looking up at the turn of the century, when the Mariinsky system had been renovated, but Vytegra was still as remote and provincial as ever and, like many such towns in the Russian Empire, even served as a place of exile. Vytegra had to wait for a few more decades until, in the 1950s and 1960s, the construction and opening of the Volga-Baltic waterway system gave it new life and its population trebled to 12,000.

The appearance of the old part of the town is largely determined by the buildings from the late 18th and early 19th century which, owing to the years of stagnation when there was little construction work, still stand intact. Originally the property of well-to-do merchants, they are typically two-storeyed stone mansions built in the classical style.

A number of Vytegra's historical monuments are related to the Mariinsky system. When the Volga-Baltic system was being constructed, one old wooden lock was preserved as a kind of museum piece, complete with all its hand-operated machinery. This lock, on the left

64. Kizhi Island: the Veronica Chapel (17th-18th century) from the village of Vigovo. It was erected on the site of the Chapel of the Holy Ghost, property of the Yamka villagers, which burnt down shortly after the war. Standing on the crest of Naryina Hill, Kizhi's highest point, it commands a spectacular view of the island.

bank, has tarred walls and a lifting gate and is a perfect piece of early Russian hydro-engineering, at one time the most advanced in the whole of Europe. Next to the lock stands a tiny wooden building that used to house an electric power station. In 1982, it was reopened as the Volga-Baltic Museum, with exhibits relating the story of the Mariinsky system and the Volga-Baltic waterway. The tall obelisk nearby commemorates the opening of the New Mariinsky Canal in 1886.

The local ethnography museum is accommodated in the Church of the Purification of the Virgin (1869-1873), built to commemorate the centenary of the town's foundation. This monumental five-domed edifice in the Russian-Byzantine style was designed by A. Chetverukhin, chief architect of Olonets Province. It is perched on Krasnaya Gorka (Red Hill), the highest point of the left bank, and dominates the town's skyline as seen from the river. The museum's best sections are those of folk arts and crafts and old Russian painting from the area east of Lake Onega. The museum's special feature is a collection of models of various architectural monuments in the area that were made by a local craftsman, Y.G. Tverdov.

Not far from the ethnography museum stands a chapel that was moved here from its original site on Besednaya Gora. This unusual cruciform structure built of massive logs has a lavishly ornamented roof fringe. Though not exactly ancient—it dates from 1881—the chapel demonstrates the continuity of the time-honoured wood-carving skills of the area.

Those interested in folk crafts may like to look at the pottery of the

65. Kizhi is both an architectural and an ethnographic museum. Its dwelling houses and outbuildings give an idea of the daily life of Russian and Karelian peasants in the Onega area. In summer the Kizhi Museum invites folk dancers and singers and also skilled needlewomen, weavers, woodcarvers and potters, to recreate the atmosphere of the past.

village of Andoma, some 30 kilometres north of Vytegra on the road to Pudozh. The heydey of this centuries-old craft was in the early 20th century, when local potters manufactured earthenware, clay vases, various small articles and amusing figurines. The ethnography museum in Vytegra keeps a fine collection of these items.

The Canals. The most famous of the ancient trade routes between the Baltic and the Black and Caspian seas, the way 'from the Varangians to the Greeks', went upstream along the rivers flowing into the Baltic Sea and then continued south along the Volga and the Dnieper. Many of the rivers, the main communication routes, were connected by portage tracks, on which boats were dragged overland from one river to another. The Russian word for portage, *volok*, is incorporated in a number of place names, such as the town of Volokolamsk in Moscow Region and Vyshny Volochok in Tver Region. After the emergence of the unified Russian state, and particularly from the reign of Peter the Great, ties between Russia's central areas and the Baltic lands acquired added significance. It was thus essential that the Volga, Russia's number-one trade and transportation artery, should be linked to the Baltic Sea.

The earliest navigable system of canals connecting St Petersburg, the new capital of Russia, with the Volga basin and all the central parts of the country was the Vyshny Volochok system, built at the beginning of the 18th century, linking a Volga tributary, the Tvertsa, and the Msta River, which flows into Lake Ilmen, with the Volkhov River, Lake

Ladoga and the Neva. The town of Vyshny Volochok in Tver Region,
where the main canal and reservoir system were built, remains a monument to 18th-century hydro-engineering. In the early 19th century two
more hydro-systems between the Baltic and the Volga were put into
operation, almost simultaneously; one was the Tikhvin, linking up the
Chagoda and the Sias River flowing into Lake Ladoga; the other was
the Mariinsky, joining together the Kovzha and the Vytegra that flows
into Lake Onega. The Vyshny Volochok system gradually fell into disuse, navigation being hampered by rapids in the Msta and the Volkhov,
and by the start of the 20th century it had been closed altogether.

The Tikhvin navigation system, completed in 1811, was fairly
important throughout the first half of the 19th century, when it served
for shipping goods from St Petersburg to the famous Volga fairs in
Nizhny Novgorod and Makariev. However, the construction of a railway
line in the area robbed it of most of its trade, and in 1965 it was closed.

The Mariinsky system came into operation in 1810, a century after
Peter the Great conceived the idea of connecting his new capital on the
Neva with the Volga by means of a canal joining the Kovzha and the
Vytegra. In 1710 the surveying work was entrusted to a Scottish engin-
eer, John Perry, and the following year Peter the Great personally visited the watershed between the two rivers and spent several days wan-
dering about the forests and marshes there, accompanied by local peasants. Finally, the monarch indicated the place where the canal was to be
dug. But this was as far as it got: nothing more was done at the time
and Peter's successors forgot all about the project. It was not until the

68. *Every church and chapel dome in Kizhi is covered with a type of wooden shingle, 'lemekh', that from a distance resembles fish scales. Each is in itself a work of art, though carpenters use nothing more sophisticated than an axe to fashion them. Thousands of pieces, each individually crafted to take account of curvature, are needed for every church.*

end of the 18th century that the idea was revived, and in 1796 work finally started. As often happens, the main obstacle was lack of money in the treasury, so Tsar Paul gave permission for an annual 'loan' of 400,000 rubles from the fund of the St Petersburg Orphanage. As the orphans' home was under the patronage of Tsaritsa Maria Fedorovna, the new navigation system was named Mariinsky in her honour.

Its construction lasted for fifteen years. Besides the actual canal, numerous other hydro-engineering works had to be built, with a large number of locks. Soon after navigation started, it became apparent that the system fell short of expectations—transhipments had to be made throughout the way and storms on the lakes occasionally resulted in shipwrecks—so a bypass canal was duly dug (1845-1852) along the southern shore of Lake Onega. From the 1860s on, the Mariinsky system underwent all manner of rebuilding, and eventually had its locks and main canal drastically overhauled between 1890 and 1910.

By the standards of its time, the Mariinsky system was a first-rate piece of hydro-engineering. It was one of the foremost of its kind in the world in terms of the work scale and was actually longer than the Suez Canal and the Panama Canal built later. In the late 1930s, this vital waterway entered yet another renovation phase, but work was interrupted by the Second World War and completed only in 1964.

A trip along the old Mariinsky system took two weeks; today a passenger boat covers the distance between Lakes Beloe and Onega in a single night. Thanks to six giant locks, ships can negotiate the watershed between the lakes which is 80 metres above the Onega level. Now even the largest vessels sail from the Volga to the Baltic Sea, covering the 1,100 kilometres between the Volga and St Petersburg along an intricate network of rivers, lakes, canals and reservoirs.

Lake Onega. Fifteen kilometres downstream from the town of Vytegra, the river flows into Onega, Europe's second largest freshwater lake (9,610 sq. km.). It is part of the vast lake district in Karelia and Finland stretching from the Gulf of Finland and the Gulf of Bothnia in the Baltic Sea all the way to the White Sea. The further north one travels, the more dramatic is the scenery; in places the rocky cliffs that rise above the water carry petroglyphs made in the second millennium B.C. by the ancestors of Finnic tribes, the ancient inhabitants of these parts. The eastern and northern shores of the lake are sparsely populated; this is the ideal place for fishing and mushroom and berry gathering in the virgin coniferous forests.

From the Vytegra estuary in the south, ships cross Onega to its northern part, where its shores are indented with numerous bays and inlets, and its waters dotted with hundreds of islands of every conceivable shape and size. The lake, in fact, has 1,650 islands all told.

Kizhi Island, the northernmost point of the White Nights Voyage, can also be reached by travelling by rail or road to Petrozavodsk, whence hydrofoils make regular trips to the island during the navigation season (taking less than two hours each way).

The island is eight kilometres long from its northern to its southern tip, but just a few minutes' walk across. Its chief claim to fame is its set of wooden buildings, most from the 18th century, though structures of similar type stood here in far more distant times. The island's name derives from the Karelian word *kizhat* meaning 'playground', that is, the site of pagan rites. Later, with the advent of Orthodox Christianity, Kizhi retained its religious significance, and when a church had been erected there, it became a *pogost*, or parish centre.

69. *The buildings (overleaf) of the Kizhi parish centre ('pogost'): a bell-tower (1860-1870), the Transfiguration Church (1714) and the Intercession Church (1764).*

70. The Transfiguration Church on Kizhi Island. Its 22 domes (no other church can boast of so many) ascend the body of the church to the height of 37 metres. The Kizhi churches are believed to have been originally constructed without the use of a single nail, simply by fitting the pieces together perfectly.

Karelians, the denizens of these parts, received baptism en masse in 1227. The parish was first mentioned in the chronicles under the name of Kizhi in 1496, when the land had been finally incorporated in the Russian state. In the mid-17th century, the parish of Kizhi had about 130 villages with a total of over 11,000 inhabitants.

In the middle of the 17th century, the government placed on the local peasants the duty of guarding border villages against Swedish incursions. Twice the Kizhi parish saw peasant revolts—in 1695 and from 1769 to 1771 (the latter uprising is commemorated by a plaque by the entrance to the *pogost* premises). Both times the disturbances were provoked by the government's orders to send the parish people to work at the Olonets iron foundries and by their consequent impoverishment. The Transfiguration and Intercession churches of Kizhi were mentioned for the first time in 1616, but both were struck by lightning and burnt down at the close of the 17th century. Soon after, work began on the architectural ensemble that can be seen in Kizhi today.

The area around Onega is a treasury of old wooden architecture. Small wonder, too: in the last century the 275,000-strong population of Olonets Province had at their disposal 594 churches, 18 monasteries and 1,724 prayer houses and chapels!

Beautiful wooden buildings are not the only thing to admire here; these parts are also a repository of folklore and oral literature. Many famous folk story-tellers and poets lived in the vicinity of Kizhi, and their gift was passed on from generation to generation. Trofim Riabinin (1791-1885), founder of a whole dynasty of story-tellers, was buried in the Kizhi *pogost* graveyard. His son, Ivan Riabinin (1844-1908), performed not only in Russia—in Moscow, St Petersburg, Odessa and Kiev—but also in Serbia, Bulgaria and Austria-Hungary, and some of his chants were used by the composer Rimsky-Korsakov. Irina Fedosova (1831-1899), another native of the Kizhi area, was much admired by Chaliapine and the writer Maxim Gorky. The latter testified that she knew 30,000 verses by heart! A few of the stories narrated by another Kizhi story-teller, Vassily Shcheglenok (1805-1894), inspired the great Lev Tolstoi himself!

From 1941 to 1944, Kizhi Island was occupied by Finnish troops and the Intercession Church was reopened to hold services for the soldiers. Among the Finnish contingent was a young researcher, Lars Petersson, who later made a valuable contribution to the study of wooden architecture in the eastern Onega area.

Currently, there are a mere 40 people living in the two inhabited villages on the island. Kizhi is now a historical, architectural and ethnographic reserve, established in the 1950s and 1960s, when the monuments it already possessed were augmented by fine examples of wooden architecture from nearby villages on other islands and the shores of Lake Onega, carefully reassembled on the new site.

Wooden churches and chapels. The centrepiece of the Kizhi ensemble is the majestic, multi-domed Transfiguration Church, built in 1714 and unequalled by anything in Russia. According to legend, when it was completed, the masterbuilder Nestor, who with his team had created this miracle with nothing but ordinary axes for tools, flung his axe into the lake, saying: 'There has not been, is not and will never be another such church.' Indeed, one cannot help marvelling at the graceful ease with which the 22 cupolas of the Transfiguration Church run up its tapering frame—no other church ever had as many domes.

The three-dimensional composition of the church is not really complex, for all its seeming intricacy. Its basic element is a great octa-

71. Oshevnev's house (19th century) on Kizhi, a peasant dwelling fairly typical of the Onega area. By combining the living quarters and farm buildings under a single roof, it enabled its inhabitants to spend weeks indoors during the long and bitterly cold northern winters without once going outside.

hedral log frame with four tall, two-level extensions facing east, west, north and south to form a cross. The octahedron is surmounted by two tiers of smaller octahedrons, the upper one crowned with an onion dome. The interior of the Transfiguration Church is graced with a four-tier carved iconostasis from the mid-18th century with icons of the 17th and 18th centuries, their colours as rich and vivid as ever.

All *pogosts* in the north typically had two churches—one heated, for winter, the other unheated, for summer use. In keeping with this practice, next to the big church the smaller Intercession Church was built as Kizhi's winter place of worship (some experts date it to 1764, others to the early 18th century). Summer churches were usually more richly ornamented, larger and taller, warmth not being the builders' primary concern. One can only admire the instinct and talent of the nameless craftsmen who placed the second church in such a way that neither edifice rivalled and overshadowed the other. The Intercession Church seems to echo its peerless neighbour and complements it to make up a perfect ensemble.

Particularly effective is the upper part of the church with its central dome and eight smaller cupolas clustered around it. An important decorative element is the openwork carved band encircling the top of the building like a festive collar. This is characteristic of Onega churches and a hallmark of local architecture. The original interior decoration of the Intercession Church has been lost; it now has has a set of 17th- and 18th-century icons collected from villages in the area.

Summer churches built of wood have better chances of survival than their winter, heated, counterparts: the logs used in their construction did not have to be caulked with moss or oakum, there was less damp inside (as moisture did not condense there during colder seasons) and the ventilation was better.

In the 1860s and 1870s, a team of carpenters headed by peasant Sisoi Petrukhin of Pudozh built the 30-metre bell-tower to replace an earlier bell-tower that had to be pulled down because of its advanced state of decay. The new bell-tower bears some resemblance to urban stone architecture of the second half of the 19th century.

The three tall edifices, visible from miles away, are said to have served as a kind of beacon for peasants from nearby villages who sailed to the island to pray. Even though they differ in size and age, they make a uniquely harmonious whole.

It is amazing how the Kizhi miracle managed to survive the endless upheavals of history: peasant uprisings, the Civil War, the violent anti-religious campaign of the 1920s and 1930s, the Second World War.... Possibly, because of the island's remote position, it simply had the good fortune to be ignored and forgotten for years. Kizhi was 'rediscovered' after the Second World War, when teams of architects and restorers started coming here. In the 1960s, Kizhi became a popular media subject and ever since has attracted thousands of tourists.

For a century and a half both churches were 'clad' in weatherboarding—in accordance with the 19th-century 'fashion'—and it was not until 1959 that they could be viewed in their original splendour. The walls of churches and of virtually all other buildings in the north were made of pine logs shaped with an axe, the only tool used by carpenters until the second half of the last century, though they were also familiar with the saw, of course. An axe-hewn log will keep better than sawn timber: pores at the ends of logs get clogged sufficiently to keep out the moisture, and the wood does not rot away. The annual rings on the logs used for building help reconstruct the history of old monuments, while analysis of the wood enables researchers to date the building itself, for the exact year of construction is hardly ever recorded.

They say the Kizhi churches were originally built without a single nail, the parts ideally fitted together. (Note that each church, besides the structural elements, had thousands, if not tens of thousands, of purely ornamental pieces.) Even if the 'no nails' story is just a local myth, this does nothing to diminish one's admiration for the remarkable engineering ingenuity and skill of the builders. A fair proportion of the details of the Transfiguration and Intercession Churches, including some of the ornamental features, actually serve to remove excess water from the roofs and domes, or form part of the ventilation system that allows the wood to 'breathe' and so escape rot and decay. For instance, the cascade of domes on the Transfiguration Church is no idle quirk of the builders' imagination, argue some experts, but a perfect system of damp protection: the domes have been ideally placed to suit the purpose of rainwater drainage.

The domes of every church and chapel on Kizhi are covered with a kind of shingle: numerous shaped pieces of wood that, from a distance, resemble fish scales and are known to Russian carpenters as *lemekh*. Each in itself is a triumph of carpentry, and there are thousands on every church (the Transfiguration Church alone took tens of thousands!). The *lemekh* coating of domes was done in overlapping rows, starting from the bottom. The right wood for making *lemekh* is aspen: not only is it damp-resistant, but when ageing it acquires a noble silvery sheen which changes its shade as it catches the light. Depending on the time of day and the weather, the *lemekh*-covered

Kizhi domes now appear black, now glow like copper, shimmer like burnished silver or take on a strange, ponderous leaden look.

At the time of cruel wars in the 17th century, the *pogost* of Kizhi was protected by a stout wall, which still existed in the 18th century, as can be seen in an old engraving. The low wooden paling that surrounds the *pogost* today was added in 1959 in imitation of certain wooden structures still found in the North. Apart from the main ensemble of the Kizhi *pogost*, there are several dozen other examples of northern wooden architecture on the island.

The Church of the Resurrection of Lazarus, the oldest building on the island, was brought over from the Murom Monastery on the southeastern shore of Lake Onega and erected to the south of the central ensemble of Kizhi in 1959. The building is tiny (just 8.8 m. long, 3.6 m. wide and 5.4 m. high) and modestly decorated, but the little church is of exceptional interest as one of Russia's oldest surviving architectural monuments made of wood. Legend has it that the church was built in the lifetime of the Reverend Lazarus, founder of the Murom Monastery, who died in 1391 aged one hundred and five. According to legend, Lazarus was born in Constantinople (traditionally referred to in Russia as the 'Second Rome') and visited Novgorod twice, on the orders of the Constantinople Patriarch. Eventually he settled in the Novgorod area and did missionary work in its more remote parts, east of Lake Onega, where he founded the monastery first mentioned by the chronicles in 1352. In the second half of the 19th century the little church was an object of pilgrimage: rumours of its 'miraculous heal-

ing powers' attracted crowds of believers. In 1885-1886, the monastery builders even put up a wooden case around the church to preserve the valuable relic.

The Chapel of the Archangel Michael, brought over from the village of Lelikozero (32 km. north of Kizhi), is typical of the chapels built all over the Russian North and the Onega area in the 18th century. Though all very similar, no two of them were exactly alike. The chapels erected in various parts of the island serve as landmarks for strolling visitors. Naryinsky Hill in the northern part, which is the island's highest highest point, is surmounted by the Veronica Chapel (17th and 18th centuries) from the village of Vigovo. Its graceful outline blending into the scenery to perfection can be seen from all sides and, like the main Kizhi ensemble, has become one of the island's architectural motifs.

The Chapel of the Three High Priests from the village of Kavgora, which stands close to the northern tip of the island, is one of the most beautiful pieces in this outdoor museum's architectural collection. In contrast to all the other buildings brought there, the Kavgora chapel (17th-18th century) is an example of Karelian architecture. Beside the Chapel of the Three High Priests, standing 25 metres high and strikingly bold in design, any other chapel on Kizhi looks modest.

Approaching the village of Vassilievo, two kilometres north of the *pogost* on the western shore of the island, the shapely form of the Assumption Chapel, nestling in a hollow there, can be seen from afar. Built in the 17th and 18th centuries, the chapel is a tripartite structure comprising an enclosed porch, a refectory and the chapel proper.

75. The Chapel of the Archangel Michael (18th century), brought to Kizhi from the village of Lelikozero. Inside there are interesting old paintings of archangels on 12 panels and of the Creator within the central circle.

Several other villages around the island also have interesting chapels that make up what is known as the Kizhi Necklace. Before the ship reaches Kizhi, passengers can already see the Chapel of the Virgin's Sign (18th century) in the village of Korba, standing on the very edge of the low shore, almost hidden in a fir-tree grove on Greater Klimetsky Island. Right next to Korba is another village, Vorobyi, where the hilltop Chapel of St Kirik and St Ulita (late 18th-early 19th century) is silhouetted against the sky. Further away, in Podielniki (which means 'Village Under the Firs'), the tiny, toy-like Chapel of St Parasceva and St Varlaam of Khutyn (19th century), like something out of a fairy-tale, peeps out behind an enclosure of mossy boulders among giant firs. The builders in the village of Volkostrov must have had other ideas about the proper site for a chapel, for the Chapel of St Peter and St Paul (17th-18th century) stands in the open, for the whole village to admire. Besides all the usual ornamental elements in carved wood, it has a projecting gallery with a finely carved balustrade on its southern façade.

Village life and homesteads. There was a time when Kizhi, along with the nearby islands, was far more densely populated. Every bit of arable land was meticulously tilled and planted with cereals: the Onega shore is one of the few places in Karelia where wheat can be grown. The local soil, which turns into clouds of grey dust on a dry, warm day and into black mud in the rain, is known as *shungisite* (after the township of Shunga in Karelia). It is said to have excellent warmth-

retaining properties, thanks to which wheat manages to ripen here. Kizhi still bears some traces of the back-breaking work needed to grow wheat in these parts. Before sowing could start, the field had to be cleared of thousands of stones, but the very next spring it would be liberally covered with a new lot. Quite a few local children are still convinced that stones 'grow' from the earth. In this way the former fields eventually acquired their skirting of *rovnitsi*—rows of neat piles of stones that form a wall. These memorials to the diligence of local farmers are now admired by all who come to Kizhi.

The villages on Kizhi, and generally in Karelia and in the North of Russia, are often small and compact. Many consist of just a single homestead, a kind of fortress which used to protect its inhabitants from the vicissitudes of weather and united under its roof not merely a family but a whole clan, often of 20 to 30 people of four generations. The core structure was a dwelling of one or two storeys with a cluster of sheds and barns for storing grain and fodder and for sheltering the livestock during winter months. As the family grew and living conditions became increasingly cramped, more extensions were built and more storeys added, but usually all under the same roof. The result was an enormous rambling structure housing livestock, storage premises and workshops as well as having numerous living rooms, some of which could be heated (*izba*), while others were used mostly in summer and had no stoves (*gornitsa, svetelka*). Sometimes there would also be a number of detached outbuildings: granaries, sheds, threshing barns or bath-houses.

This practice of building extended homesteads is attributed to the strong family ties and severe weather conditions—even in the cruellest of winters, when the earth was buried under three feet of snow and the temperature dropped to 40 degrees below freezing, people could tend their livestock and manufacture things without venturing more than a few steps outside.

The first floor of the living quarters in these 'peasant castles' is skirted by an open gallery (*gulbishche*), which has a utilitarian function, giving access to the windows from the outside for closing the

77. The Kizhi skerries (overleaf) are a legacy of the glacier that retreated northwards clawing the earth on the way, as it were. That is why all the narrow straits and islands in Lake Onega lie on a north-south axis. The farther north, the more numerous the islands, and the more rugged the shoreline.

shutters, but at the same time imparts a festive look. Intricate wood-carving decorates all the window frames and the friezes around the roof, which are reminiscent of openwork embroidery. The patterns mostly run to various combinations of the cross within a circle, in which the solar image from the pagan past is easily recognisable.

This type of house continued to be built in the North till the early 1900s. But unlike churches and chapels, houses were frequently rebuilt and extended, or sometimes pulled down altogether, depending on the family's needs. The owners often did the job themselves, for every farmer in the North was of necessity a skilled carpenter. As a result, one would be hard put to it now to find a dwelling older than the 19th century, but since the building techniques and architecture of farm-houses do not easily yield to change, even relatively new examples can be regarded as monuments of a folk building craft many centuries old.

Perhaps the most interesting of the peasant houses on Kizhi is Oshevnev's house (19th century). This two-storeyed building, fairly typical of the Onega farmstead, consists of a stout, rectangular structure made of heavy logs and covered with a ridge roof, flanked on one side by a spacious extension with a gently sloping roof, used for all kinds of farmwork. The house measures 22 metres in length, and 18 in width. Its total floor space is 396 square metres, of which 143 are taken up by the living quarters. In 1876 it was occupied by a family of 22 members! Apart from its impressive size, Oshevnev's house is remarkable for its richly ornamented façade, a feature of 19th-century wooden architecture in the North that shows the influence of metropolitan architectural styles.

The great logs of the house walls set off the magnificent carving of the *prichelinas* (decorative boards fixed to the front of a wooden building to conceal the butts of the roofing) and *polotentse* ends (over-hanging *prichelina* sections). Even more beautiful carving, every fragment a little work of art, decorates the window frames and shutters with their figural tops and the *gulbishche* around the first floor. The main façade overlooking the lake has a mezzanine with a dainty little balcony, also beautifully carved. Similar balconies nestle under the eaves on either side of the house. Their purpose must have been chiefly ornamental, for none have doors opening onto them, only fairly narrow windows through which only a particularly slender and agile individual could hope to squeeze.

Somewhat more modest, both in size and decoration, is the Yelizarov house (1880s) from the village of Seredka on Greater Klimetsky Island. Of a different type is the Yakovlev house (end of the 19th century) from the Karelian village of Kleshcheila, in which all the components lie along the same axis. The façade lavishly decorated with wood carvings is not unlike the decor of Oshevnev's house, though the patterns here are markedly Karelian.

Of the eleven villages on Kizhi as recently as the 19th century (in the 1920s the island's population totalled 250), only two have survived. Vassilievo, by the old wooden pier, has three houses. One of them, the large two-storeyed Sergin house with a mezzanine (1880-1890), unoccupied today, was moved to the island from the village of Munozero in 1972. Visible from afar as one approaches Kizhi in a boat, the house stands farther back from the shore than its neighbours, which seem about to wade into the lake, and on a higher level, so that it appears to soar above the other buildings.

The houses in the village of Yamka on the opposite side of the island are quite large by local standards and all inhabited. Each one is a museum piece surviving largely intact from the last century. On

78. Round Square in
Petrozavodsk has preserved the
city's only set of buildings in the
classical style (mid-1770s),
comprising six administration
buildings of Olonets factories
with two annexes that were
rebuilt in the 1780s in semicir-
cular blocks to house the local
government bodies. The monument to Lenin in the square (by
M.G. Manizer), made of 14
granite blocks and 11 metres
high, is one of the biggest Lenin
monuments in Russia. (See p. 112)

raised ground some way off stands the worship cross from the village
of Khashezero (early 19th century), one of the typical features of a
northern village. Its decorative rosettes still carry the date '1812' and
the legend 'Victory': the war against Napoleon had its impact even in
this remote part of Russia.

No less striking than the dwelling houses are the farm outbuildings—both the original Kizhi pieces and the later additions to its museum collection brought from other places. True, they are devoid of ornamental carving, but the grim solidity of their stout walls is quite
impressive in itself. A vital part of any farmstead is the granary, where
the fruits of the family's yearly toil in the fields are stored. Granaries
were a highly valued property and were usually placed at a safe distance from the house as a precaution against fire.

Another necessary and traditional item at a farmstead was the
bath-house. Inside was an open stone hearth (*kamenka*) with no chim-
ney: the smoke escaped through the open door and holes left in the ceil-
ing. This method of heating had been known from very early times as
kurnoi (from the word *kurit*, 'to smoke'), the name which is still used
for this type of rural bath-house in the North. The Kizhi bath-houses,
at Yamka, for instance, are still used for ablutions: in the late afternoon,
especially before a weekend or a holiday, smoke can often be seen curl-
ing over the squat little houses by the lake.

Many villages in the Onega area had their own flour mills, both
the water- and the wind-powered varieties. The former is represented
by the mill from the village of Berezovaya Selga (1875), the latter by

79. Monument to Peter the Great, the founder of Petrozavodsk, the work of sculptor I.N. Schroeder and architect I.A. Monighetti, erected in 1872 to mark the bicentenary of the Emperor's birth. The pedestal is of grey granite quarried near the town of Sortavala in Karelia.

80. Bread is Russia's staple food and its per capita consumption here is greater than anywhere else in the world. In villages, much of the daily fare, such as milk and potatoes, is locally produced. Bread, however, is usually bought in bakeries.

81. The Resurrection Church at Kurpovo, near the village of Vazhiny, stands on the site of two earlier wooden churches burnt down during the wars with the Poles and Swedes. The legend in Old Slavonic lettering on its iconostasis states: 'In the year 7138 (1630 by the Gregorian calendar) on the 26th day of September was this temple created.' The Kurpovo 'pogost' was both a religious and an administrative centre and Vazhiny was famous for its nine-day fairs. (See p. 115)

the windmill from the village of Volkostrov (1928).

Some of the Kizhi houses have been converted into small museums to give an idea of the daily life of Onega peasants in the 19th century; they also display some of the more unusual articles made by local craftsmen.

The interior of a northern house is a world to itself. When you cross the porch and step over the high threshold, you enter a spacious anteroom through a relatively narrow door (both the high threshold and the width of door were necessary to conserve heat in winter). The anteroom connects the main parts of the homestead: its living quarters and the farm buildings. The former were typically two-storeyed, with the ground floor often used for storage purposes, though normally part of it was lived in. The main living area was always a room with a fireplace called the *izba*.

The farm premises attached to the house were likewise on two levels, with the livestock kept on the ground floor and the upper level (*povet*) used to store hay and various equipment, such as fishing nets, fishing and hunting tackle, etc. The *povet* could be reached either from inside the house, through the anteroom, or from the outside, by a sturdy, ramp-like structure of logs that led straight to the second level and could easily support a horse-drawn cart or sledge.

The furnishings of the Onega house, like the outside decoration, depended largely on how well-to-do the owners were, but in any case tended to be simple and of a traditional type. The lack of space was another limiting factor, so household articles were kept to a minimum.

82. The Chapel of St Peter and St Paul (17th-18th century) in the village of Zaozerie is of the type known as a 'klet' church: a rectangular frame covered by a ridge roof, which is similar to the common peasant house ('klet'). (See p. 117)

The very heart of the northern house is the large closed fireplace, without which life would be simply impossible. Besides its use for heating and cooking, it is also a bed for young children and old folk, and a bath tub for infants (babies were bathed in the oven!). Since night sets in early in the North in winter, the afternoon housework had to be done by the light of burning splinters. Though towards the end of the 19th century villagers in the Onega country were already familiar with paraffin lamps, paraffin was too expensive a commodity to oust splinter lighting. The splinter was fixed in a finely forged iron holder known as *svetets*, which would be placed over a hand basin or a tub filled with water so that the burnt particles that fell off were not a fire hazard.

Most of the items that can now be seen in Kizhi peasant homes were made by their owners themselves or else by some fellow-villager. Predictably, the most popular material for their manufacture was wood, being by far the most accessible and easy to fashion. Virtually every part of the tree was used to make one household article or another: the trunk, the bark, warts, roots and branches. For instance, scoops, mortars and bowls were normally made of tree warts, a type of excrescence with particularly tough and durable tissue. Articles made of warts can last ages, and their shape is pleasantly rounded and easy to work with.

Birch bark was another favourite material that found innumerable uses, from baskets and cases for whetstones to salt-cellars and purses. A *tues* stitched from a single piece of birch bark was good for keeping milk in: birch bark has excellent insulating qualities and milk would stay fresh even on the hottest of days. Birch-bark containers were also

83. St Nicholas's Church in the village of Sogintsi (1696), proudly referred to by local people as 'the Sogintsi wonder'. Unlike most other architectural monuments in the region, it has survived largely unaltered and has preserved intact an unusual vernacular building style. The church is 32 metres in height and constructed of enormous fir and larch logs. Standing on a sort of peninsula formed by a twist of the Vazhinka River, it can be seen from afar. (See p. 115)

convenient for keeping salt, grain and flour in; being waterproof, they prevented those substances from getting damp.

The amount of relatively rare copperware was a reliable indicator of the household's affluence. Bulbous samovars, mortars and pestles had to be bought and were much more expensive than wooden articles or earthenware. Accordingly, these 'status symbols' would be burnished till they shone and kept in a prominent place.

The *izba* corner with an icon, invariably draped with an embroidered towel, was its most honoured part. It was called the 'red corner' (the Russian word *krasny*, 'red', also means 'beautiful', 'festive', 'the best'). In Onega houses this is usually the corner in the far right-hand part of the room, diagonally across from the fireplace. Respected visitors were seated here, under the saints' images.

Karelian houses have always been noted for their scrupulous cleanliness. On Saturdays all the floors, tables and benches were washed and scrubbed without fail, window panes and rows of wall logs were wiped clean. Floors and ceilings were left unpainted; before each holiday they were just scraped white.

Kizhi does not have a hotel, but anyone who will take the trouble to arrange this with the management of the Kizhi Museum beforehand may be sure of accommodation for the night in one of the little guest houses on the eastern shore. A walk along Kizhi at dusk is a rare pleasure. At sunset, while the summer sun takes its time over sinking out of sight, the Kizhi monuments are at their best. The most memorable view of the island is from the Veronica Chapel.

ALONG THE SVIR RIVER

84, 85. St Athanasius's Chapel (18th century) in the village of Posad. The area around the River Svir is a perfect treasury of Russian wooden architecture. Podporozhie District alone boasts 64 wooden buildings— mainly churches and chapels— of historical and architectural interest. (See p. 117)

Petrozavodsk, Karelia's capital, on the western shore of Lake Onega, is a port of call for most cruises between Moscow and St Petersburg. As for those who travel by train or by car, they simply cannot miss the city on their way to Kizhi.

The birth of Petrozavodsk is closely connected with the activities of Peter the Great. The Great Northern War between Russia and Sweden then in progress required a powerful military industry. Karelia's rich deposits of iron and copper ores were the starting point for building a number of foundries there. When the largest of these, the Petrovsky works (*zavod* in Russian), was put into operation in 1703, a few clusters of houses for the workers sprang up around it on the lake shore. By 1777 the settlement had grown into the township of Petrozavodsk and was given civic status. In 1782, it was already the main city of the newly established Olonets Province. However, throughout the 19th century Petrozavodsk remained markedly provincial, with just 10,000 inhabitants, and only the construction of the Murmansk railway line in the early 1900s finally encouraged it to burgeon. The original works founded by Peter the Great is still there, though now it is the Onega tractor plant. Petrozavodsk today is a major modern city and port with a population of 300,000.

On the Onega shore, not far from the boat station, there is a monument to Peter the Great, the city's founder. Another prominent feature of the city is the administration buildings in Kruglaya (Round) Square. Two other places that should not be missed are the Karelian Ethnography Museum and the Karelian Museum of Fine Arts.

The visitor may be surprised by all the inscriptions in the Latin alphabet to be seen in Petrozavodsk. Karelia has two official languages, Russian and Karelian, and the latter employs Finnish for its written form. The city boasts a Finnish drama theatre, the only one in Russia.

From Petrozavodsk one can take a trip to Martsialnie Vodi (65 km.), Russia's oldest watering place, built around a mineral spring in 1719 on the orders of Peter the Great, and named after Mars, the Roman god of war. Another interesting excursion place (75 km. away) is the Kivach waterfall on the Suna River, one of the biggest lowland waterfalls in Europe (11 m. high).

The Svir River. From Lake Onega, the ship enters the Svir (224 km.), which flows into Ladoga. The river once had numerous rapids that made navigation difficult, but now that the water level has been considerably raised by the construction of two hydro-systems, these are no longer a hazard.

Close to the source of the Svir is the township of Voznesenie (Ascension), which took its name from the Ascension Monastery, long since dissolved. The township owes its origin in 1852 to the building of the Onega bypass canal that reached the Vytegra and allowed smaller vessels to avoid Lake Onega. The strategically placed township grew rapidly, and by 1900 had 1,100 inhabitants. During the navigation season, over 4,000 cargo vessels laden with timber, flour and other commodities called at the Voznesenie landing carrying almost 30 million rubles' worth of goods (a vast sum at the time). About 11,000 tons of building timber alone were shipped annually from here to St Petersburg and other cities.

After the Volga-Baltic deep-water navigation system had been built, Voznesenie retained its role of a river and lake port: freighters go from here westwards to St Petersburg, eastwards to Vytegra and from there on to the Upper Volga, or northwards to Petrozavodsk, whence they can reach the White Sea by the White Sea-Baltic Canal. The township's distinctive feature is its wooden pavements, which were once common in the Russian North.

Podporozhie is the largest population centre by the upper reaches of the Svir. The town can be reached by train from Moscow or St Petersburg to Murmansk and Petrozavodsk, and by car from St Petersburg (260 km.), Vytegra (160 km.) and Moscow (730 km., via Tver and Lodeinoe Pole).

First mentioned in 1496, the locality was alternately referred to as Pogra and Podporozhie. Rapids (Russian *porog*) dotted the entire length of the Svir river-bed from Voznesenie on, and the one considered the most hazardous, the Bear Rapid, was slightly upstream of present-day Podporozhie, hence the name the town finally settled for, meaning 'place below the rapid'. It discarded its other name after 1703, when Peter the Great ordered peasants from Novgorod Province to be resettled here to pilot vessels through the rapids. Boats going upstream were towed by teams of horses that followed the well-beaten track along the bank. In the mid-19th century, even steamers negotiated the rapids here with considerable difficulty.

Podporozhie Volost (a small administrative unit) was among the poorest in Olonets Province. Farmers could not earn enough from the land to keep their families fed and clothed, so in summer local people took jobs on the river, servicing navigation, and in winter supplemented their incomes by hunting in the forests. In 1900 there were no more than 530 people living in Podporozhie. In the Second World War, the area was the site of fierce fighting.

Podporozhie was given civic status in 1956 and is now a district centre in Leningrad Region, with a population of around 30,000. Cruise liners stop here for the sole purpose of passing through the lock, as a rule, but the town has its tourist attractions and repays a closer examination. Several of the small villages in the district, on either side of the Svir, have very handsome monuments of wooden architecture, not quite as famous as the Kizhi collection, but certainly no less interesting.

There is a hotel in the town, not the height of comfort perhaps, but passable by Russian standards for a place this size. Podporozhie also has a modest ethnography museum. But the most attractive tourist sights are not in the town itself but around it, on the right and left banks of the Svir.

The river flows through densely wooded countryside: forests cover 78 per cent of Podporozhie District. In the south, among the Veps Hills, is the highest point of Leningrad Region (291 m.). Podporozhie District alone has 386 lakes of over one hectare each: the biggest are Vachozero (17 sq. km.) and Pidmozero (15.7 sq. km.). In all, water covers five per cent of the district's territory, and marshes more than 10 per cent. The forests here have an abundance of berries and also provide excellent hunting opportunities.

Villages of the Podporozhie Silver Ring. The Svir banks are fairly sparsely populated. Besides Russian settlements, there are Karelian villages to the north of the Svir and Vepsian villages to the south. The river's name itself, like most local place names, is of Finno-Ugric origin, perhaps from the word *syviri*, which in the closely related Karelian and Vepsian languages means 'deep'.

The soil here is infertile, so agriculture has never been particularly important in the local economy; the area still relies on the forest for a living. No more than five per cent of the land in the Upper Svir area is cultivated today. Villages tended to be quite small, with the exception of settlements that thrived on some river trade or craft. Numerous examples of old wooden architecture are still to be found in the countryside: all kinds of peasant houses, threshing barns, threshing floors, bath-houses and, of course, the wooden churches that were the focal points of old Novgorod *pogosts*. Building techniques and traditions from the 15th and 16th centuries were passed down from father to son, and house types remained unchanged for centuries. The many generations of craftsmen used time-perfected methods of constructing log dwellings that could last ages. They knew how to select the best site for a village, how to space farmhouses and outbuildings to advantage. Testimony of their skills can be seen in villages, both big and small, around the Svir. The wooden architecture of the Svir area has only recently begun to attract wider attention; previously, even experts were often unaware of the wealth of monuments here. Both the authorities of Podporozhie District and the local people are keen to put their part of Russia on the tourist map and will respond enthusiastically to any request for help in sightseeing.

By the source of the Vazhinka River, on the right bank of the Svir, lies the village of Vazhiny (12 km. north-west of Podporozhie). Once an important transhipment post on the trade route to the North, it even had inns and houses owned by foreign merchants. Vazhiny, mentioned

86, 87. St George's Church (1493) in Yuksovichi, built of mighty pine logs, is the oldest surviving example of wooden architecture in Leningrad Region. During the five centuries of its existence it has been more than once repaired and rebuilt. (See p. 119)

in records since the 16th century, was also famous for its autumn fairs that lasted nine days. Vazhiny *pogost* was the centre for 202 villages.

Nearby is the village of Kurpovo with the wooden Resurrection Church (1630), standing on a moderate elevation of the river bank behind a low stone wall. The church is an unusual decahedral shape and looks almost round, but in other respects is a fairly typical example of vernacular wooden architecture: it rests on a foundation of boulders and has floors of broad hewn boards. Its original appearance was somewhat altered when it was rebuilt and refurbished in the last century. The Resurrection Church consists of two churches, in fact, one for summer use and the other for winter. It has preserved its carved iconostasis from the 18th century with earlier icons. As the Resurrection Church is the only wooden church in the area where services are held, Vazhiny is at present a kind of religious centre of the district.

One more interesting wooden church of considerable age stands in the village of Sogintsi on the Vazhinka River (18 km. from Vazhiny). Villages are quite old here, four hundred years and more. In Sogintsi, all the houses are facing the river, as is usually the case in northern villages. St Nicholas's Church (1696) is a harmonious composition of a drum-like octahedral body with two extensions—a chancel and a porch—and a pyramidal bell-tower adjoining the porch. The bell-tower, estimated to be older even than the church, is most unusual: a tetrahedron of stout logs topped by a hexahedron.

St Nicholas's has survived largely intact and is now the only round, broach-roofed wooden church in an excellent state of preserva-

88, 89. The Church of the
Nativity of the Virgin (1659-
1695) in the village of Gimreka.
This interesting parish ensemble
has preserved its original low
fencing of logs with triangular
log buttresses, and a covered
gate. After restoration work
(1982-1983), the Gimreka
'pogost' assumed its original
appearance. Among the parts
carefully restored was the
wooden carving decorating the
entrance to the Nativity Church.
(See p. 120)

90. The Transfiguration Cathedral (1644), originally built of wood in 1533, was the nucleus of the Monastery of St Alexander of the Svir, the chief centre in the area for spreading Christianity among the local Veps and Karelians. Later, however, as the Valaam and Solovetsky monasteries became more famous, it lost its leading role in the north-west of Russia. (See pp. 123-127)

tion. It is an example of the so-called Ladoga style of architecture that was dominant in the areas around Ladoga and Onega and the southern part of the Olonets isthmus in the late 17th century. Inside the church, two original carved pillars support the main roof beam. All the decorative elements of the exterior imitate the usual decor of local dwelling houses. The icons from St Nicholas's Church are kept in the State Russian Museum in St Petersburg.

The village of Zaozerie, not far from Sogintsi, perched on a hill above Lake Vachozero, is notable for its interesting 17th-century Chapel of St Peter and St Paul. Originally quite small (4.2 m. by 6.9 m.), it was extended late last century: the windows were enlarged, the onion dome was shifted and a bell-tower was added. Zaozerie used to be a fairly large village and it is only in the last few decades that it has been reduced to its present depopulated state.

Next to the station of Tokari is the village of Posad with its picturesque Chapel of St Athanasius, built in the 18th century and recently renovated. In roughly the same neighbourhood, in the north of Podporozhie District (3 km. from Posad), the village of Volostnoi Navolok stands on the western shore of Lake Pidmozero (*pidm* meaning 'clogging' is another Vepsian word). Here there are two churches proudly standing on the high bank, both relics of what was once the Volostnoi Navolok *pogost*. One is the Intercession Church, built in 1783 on the site of a church of the same name first mentioned in the 16th century. The present building was probably a copy of its predecessor, for it exemplifies the oldest and most primitive type of wooden

91. Fresco in the Transfiguration Cathedral representing the vision of the Holy Trinity seen by St Alexander of the Svir prior to founding the monastery. Badly damaged during the Second World War, the monastery buildings have now been fully restored.

church: the *klet*, a simple cube of logs with a ridge roof and a pyramidal bell-tower. In 1897, when it was in a poor state of repair, it was given new weatherboarding and roofing. Apparently about the same time new windows were made in its refectory. The pyramidal bell-tower is the oldest part of the ensemble. Its west façade still has traces of a passage that was there before the existing covered passageway to the Intercession Church was built.

The winter Church of St Vlasius, slightly to the south of the older church, dates from the first half of the 19th century. Oddly enough, it is not mentioned in a single extant document, not even those referring to the fortification of the *pogost* at the end of the 19th century, so the exact year of its construction remains unknown. In the second half of the last century it was rebuilt to imitate the stone churches of the time, making it the Cinderella of the local wooden church 'community'.

The above-mentioned places form what is called the Podporozhie Silver Ring, which starts at Podporozhie and ends with the village of Pidma on the Svir River, a little upstream from Podporozhie. The route of 54 kilometres goes through Podporozhie, Vazhiny, Sogintsi, Zaozerie, Posad, Volostnoi Navolok and Pidma along macadam roads.

Yuksovichi. On the left bank of the Svir, 55 kilometres from Podporozhie on the way to Voznesenie and not far from the Podporozhie-Vytegra highway, is the village of Kishkovshchina. Situated on the shore of Lake Yuksa (12 sq. km.), which extends for seven kilometres from south-west to north-east, it is one of a cluster of

92. The Trinity ensemble of the Monastery of St Alexander of the Svir. Its main building is the masonry Trinity Cathedral (1695-1696). Next to it is a three-spired bell-tower (1647-1674); at one time the monastery bells were famous throughout Olonets Province. For many years the monastery served also as a trade centre: some 50 shops lined its walls, and the annual Trinity Fair attracted large numbers of Russian and foreign merchants.

villages known collectively as Yuksovichi. The name again has a distinctly Vepsian ring and is derived either from *yksi* ('one') or from *uks* ('door'). In the last century there were 25 tiny villages or hamlets around the lake, some with only two or three homesteads.

The pride of Yuksovichi is St George's Church (1493), the oldest monument of wooden architecture in the whole of Leningrad Region, and one of the oldest in the Russian North. The year of its construction was established in 1877 by L.V. Dahl, an expert on Russian architecture, who made a detailed study of the church. This is also basically a *klet* structure under a ridge roof. The church was smaller originally, and was rebuilt in the early 1600s to make it somewhat more spacious. It still has its old three-tier iconostasis with ancient icons grown very dark with age.

The characteristic feature of St George's Church is the series of drainage ducts projecting from under the eaves in 'herringbone' fashion, which create fascinating light-and-shade effects on the façade and at the same time prevent rainwater streaming down the steep roof from soaking the walls. According to legend, the monks who arrived at Yuksa to build a church there, rather than waste time choosing the best site, simply cast an axe handle in the water and waited for it to drift to some part of the shore and so indicate the place for them.

Gems of wooden architecture can be found in the villages north of Voznesenie, which can be reached by the road branching off from the Vytegra highway (111 km. from Podporozhie and 138 km. from

93. The Intercession Church (1619-1620), the oldest part of the Trinity complex. The feast of the Virgin's Intercession (October 14 by the Gregorian calendar), to which the church is dedicated, is a major Orthodox holiday in Russia.

Petrozavodsk). Some fifteen kilometres from Voznesenie along the Petrozavodsk highway lies the village of Shcheleiki, noted in the 18th century for its huge, colourful fairs. Above the village, half a kilometre from the Onega shore, stands the tall St Demetrius's Church, surrounded by a graveyard. Built in 1783 with money collected by the parishioners, this remarkable example of vernacular architecture belongs to the class of multi-domed wooden churches typical of the Onega area that is represented by the Kizhi masterpieces. The main part of the building is joined to the refectory and a covered passage that leads to the pyramidal bell-tower. Also of interest are the old village houses in Shcheleika with their ornamental balconies and carved window frames.

The village of Gimreka, five kilometres further on the road from Voznesenie to Petrozavodsk, also has its share of enchanting old houses. The name of the village is of Vepsian origin, related to the word *hijm* meaning 'family', 'kin'. Its showpiece is the pyramidal Church of the Nativity of the Virgin, built between 1659 and 1695 (experts disagree on the date), the centre of the Gimreka *pogost* and part of an ensemble made up of a bell-tower and a massive log fence.

94. The Intercession Church of the St Alexander of the Svir Monastery. After restoration (1969-1976), the church, badly damaged during the Second World War, regained its original 17th-century appearance and now has an airy and festive upper section with three rows of 'kokoshniks' (decorative blind arches) below the dome.

95. The Trinity Cathedral, the chief building of the monastery complex, has massive walls up to one metre thick. The tent roof is surmounted by a solitary dome that in the 19th century replaced the traditional five-dome arrangement. Some distance away is the Church of St John Damascene or Hospital Church (1716-1718).

South of the road from Podporozhie to Yuksovichi and further on to Voznesenie are the most remote villages of Leningrad Region: Shustruchei, Kuzra and Vinnitsi. The last, sprawling on the bank of the Oyat River, is considered the Vepsian 'capital', for here Veps live in a more compact group than anywhere else.

Not far from Voznesenie is the township of Shustruchei, now a composite of several old villages, rather like Yuksovichi. In its southern part, by the graveyard, stands the wooden Church of St Elijah, built in 1781 with money collected by the parishioners.

Lodeinoe Pole, where some cruise ships make a brief stop, lies sixty kilometres down the Svir from Podporozhie. It is easily accessible by rail from Moscow or St Petersburg.

The town grew out of a village called Mokrishvitsi when Peter the Great set up the Olonets shipyard there in 1702. The reasons for his choice of site were the vast forests all around that could supply timber and the Olonets foundries within easy reach that manufactured ordnance for warships. The shipyard's official name was Olonets, but it was popularly known as Lodeinoe Pole ('boat ground'), and that was

96. Valaam Island: the central complex of the Saviour Transfiguration Monastery. Valaam winters are fairly cold and whether a place can be kept warm still depends on the stock of firewood. (See p. 131)

97. View from the bell-tower of the dome of the Saviour Transfiguration Cathedral (1887-1896). The monastery workshops in the distance, once a place of bustling industrial activity, were described in the 19th-century as a 'Valaam Sheffield'.

the name eventually given to the settlement, which Catherine the Great ordered to be upgraded to the rank of town in 1785.

The Lodeinoe Pole shipyard is looked upon as the cradle of the Baltic fleet: after the fleet's first frigate, the *Standart*, over a hundred other ships were built there and took part in the naval battles of the Great Northern War. Peter I was a frequent visitor to the town, and in 1832 an obelisk in his memory was erected there by local merchants. Large vessels continued to be built at the shipyard into the 19th century. In 1818 Lodeinoe Pole launched the sloop *Mirny*, on which the explorers Mikhail Lazarev and Faddei Bellingshausen made a round-the-world voyage and discovered Antarctica. By the time the shipyard was closed in 1830, more than 450 vessels of various types had come off its slips. The town was badly damaged during the Second World War and today has virtually no historical monuments left. It is a district centre of Leningrad Region with just under 30,000 inhabitants.

Monastery of St Alexander of the Svir. North of Lodeinoe Pole, along the Olonets highway, is the village of Svirskaya Sloboda (18 km.). Here, on raised ground between lakes Roshchinskoe and

Sviatoe, is the Monastery of St Alexander of the Svir, which comprises two distinct architectural groups: the Trinity complex and the Transfiguration ensemble, half a kilometre west of the former. According to tradition, the monastery was founded in 1484 by the monk Alexander, a native of the village of Sermaksa on the Svir, who had come from the monastery on Valaam Island. He built himself a wooden cell on the shore of Lake Roshchinskoe and lived there in seclusion for seven years. In time he became one of the most revered Russian saints in the north-west of the country. According to the Life of St Alexander, the place for the monastery was not chosen at random. When he left his native village at the age of twenty-six and set off for Valaam, he stopped for the night in a forest and there had a vision of the Holy Trinity. Ten years later, Alexander made up his mind to return and settle in this place.

In 1491, the monks who had joined Alexander there built the wooden Trinity Church that formed the nucleus of the Trinity architectural complex. The Intercession Church, dating from 1533, was the first brick building raised in the monastery, using bricks made by the monks themselves. Over the next three centuries the monastery gradually acquired its final architectural physiognomy that has made it one of the more spectacular monuments of Russian architecture.

By the end of the 16th century, the Trinity ensemble had its core of brick and stone structures, while half a kilometre away, on the shore of Roshchinskoe, rose the wooden buildings of the Transfiguration complex: the cathedral, the belfry, and the dwelling and service blocks. The buildings with the monks' cells formed a courtyard and at the same time served as a protective wall. Safety was something the monks could ill afford to overlook: Polish and Swedish marauders seldom left the area alone. The Monastery of St Alexander of the Svir was ravaged three times. By far the worst was the devastation of 1618, when all the churches were destroyed and the iconostases, the library and the archives perished in the fire. When in 1641 builders began reconstructing the burnt-down Transfiguration Cathedral, they discovered the imperishable relics of St Alexander, the monastery's founder, which were subsequently placed in a silver tabernacle.

The monastery was rebuilt and expanded thanks to donations from tsars and grand dukes, and was one of the most important religious centres in the north-west of Russia. In 1703, according to tradition, Peter the Great, who had come to Lodeinoe Pole to supervise the building of the shipyard, was taken ill and spent three days at the monastery. In 1719 and 1720, he visited the cloister again, on the way to Martsialnie Vodi, this time accompanied by his wife, later Catherine I. After a fire in 1784, Catherine II the Great granted the monastery a sum of 4,000 rubles for rebuilding and renovation. Other royal visitors to the monastery were Alexander I, in 1820, and Alexander II, in 1858.

In 1779, a theological seminary opened on its premises and a number of workshops were set up. In the 19th century all the main buildings there were renovated, a house was built to accommodate pilgrims, and a water pipe was laid from Lake Roshchinskoe to the monastery. By the early 1900s, the community numbered around two hundred.

But the year 1918 was its last: a Red Army unit swooped down on the monastery, arrested all the monks, seized the valuables kept in the vestry, and carried away the relics of St Alexander from the tabernacle. Although a considerable part of the monastery valuables is stored in St Petersburg to this day, in various museums, the fate of St Alexander's relics remains unknown.

The chief building of the Trinity ensemble is the stone Trinity

Cathedral (1695-96), built on the site of the destroyed church of the same name. The majestic simplicity of its noble form, typical of the architectural style of Novgorod, sets off the elaborate ornamentation—a feature of Moscow architecture—that gives the building an air of lightness and grace. Especially interesting are the early 18th-century frescoes painted by Tikhvin masters.

South of the cathedral stands the Intercession Church, the oldest building there. The original church, built in the first half of the 16th century by one Ignaty of Moscow, was destroyed in 1618 by Swedish and Polish troops, but soon after the present church was erected in the same place. This is a tall, slender, single-domed building, square of plan, with an adjoining two-storeyed refectory surmounted by a belfry.

A rare example of 17th-century architecture is the three-tier bell-tower with wide, arched apertures, situated halfway between the Trinity Cathedral and the Intercession Church. North of the Trinity Cathedral is the Church of St John Damascene (1716-1718), otherwise known as the Hospital Church because it stood next to the monastery's infirmary. The dwelling blocks encircling the Trinity complex are also of archi-tectural interest. They were built between 1677 and 1689 to replace the

100. *Valaam: the Ascension Chapel (1912) on a hilltop over Small Nikon Bay. The area around the Resurrection and the Gethsemane hermitages were treated in the monastery as a kind of miniature Promised Land. The hill where the Resurrection Hermitage is situated, otherwise known as New Jerusalem, is called Zion; the Resurrection Chapel stands on the Mount of Olives; nearby Lake Leshchevoe was renamed the Dead Sea, and the canal linking it to Lake Sisajarvi was called the Jordan.*

101. *Valaam's northern shore. Over the centuries Lake Ladoga, while keeping the monastery isolated and inaccessible, also provided sustenance for its inhabitants. Fish, including whitefish, trout and pike perch, still abound in the lake. The monks took care to replenish its stock, every year releasing into the lake 40,000 whitefish specially bred in fish ponds.*

wooden cells destroyed by the Swedes and Poles, and have weathered the three centuries of their existence largely unaltered. Traces of the moats that at one time formed an extra line of defence are still visible.

The second monastery complex includes the Transfiguration Cathedral (1644) with the Church of St Zachariah and St Elizabeth, built on in 1668 by Maxim Semenov, 'a stonemason's apprentice from Moscow', a bell-tower and two blocks of cells. The original Transfiguration Cathedral, built of wood in 1533, burnt down in 1618. The cell blocks were completed in several stages from 1724 to 1823. The eastern block is surmounted by the Church of St Nicholas, a fairly typical piece of Russian provincial classicism of the late 18th century.

In and around the monastery there are several chapels of some interest: the stone chapel over the holy well (1780-1790)—the well, said to have been dug by St Alexander of the Svir himself, was filled up in 1700, the chapel marking the spot where Alexander had the vision of the Holy Trinity, and a delightful little wooden chapel built over a holy well by Lake Roshchinskoe.

The Svir flows into Lake Ladoga by the township of Sviritsa which, like Venice, has canals instead of streets.

130

THE HOLY ISLAND

Lake Ladoga and Valaam Island. Ladoga, Europe's largest fresh-water lake (17,700 sq. km. and 230 m. at its deepest point), is often stormy and in terms of navigation is ranked as a sea. Its southern shore is fairly even and low-lying, while the northern shore is high, rocky and deeply cut by fjords, with innumerable off-shore islands. One of these is Valaam, the largest of the fifty or so islands in the archipelago of the same name.

Valaam Monastery was for centuries among the richest, most famous and influential in Russia. According to a tradition accepted at the monastery itself, it was founded in the 10th or 11th century by a Greek monk, Sergius, and his disciple Herman, a Karelian. Another, somewhat more improbable, version claims Valaam was visited by no less than St Andrew the First-called Apostle. Most scholars agree, however, that the Valaam Monastery was founded in the 14th century, when its existence is confirmed by various historical documents.

The history of the island and monastery prior to the 18th century is both controversial and unclear, being most inadequately documented. What is certain is that the monastery, situated as it was in the border region where the interests of Novgorod Russia and Sweden continually clashed, was repeatedly ravaged by bellicose Vikings, and its monks, who preached non-resistance, were slaughtered, apart from the

105. St Nicholas's Hermitage on the island by Monastery Bay, where St Petersburg steamers used to dock, was a kind of gateway to the monastery. At one time there was a customs house here where all visitors were searched to make sure they were not trying to 'smuggle in' any liquor or tobacco, since drinking and smoking were strictly prohibited on Valaam.

106. In early winter and spring, when the lake is not navigable and the ice is dangerously thin, Valaam is virtually cut off from the rest of the world. The helicopter is the only possible means of transport, but the service is unfortunately irregular.

107. The southern end of Valaam known as the Rocky Shore. Although a canal dug in the mid-19th century and running the length of the island from north to south enters the bay here, this was always a lonely and desolate place even in the monastery's heyday.

108. The northern shore of Valaam Island, Lake Ladoga.

109. The fir and larch avenue leading to the Prior Cemetery. These tree species were introduced by the monks, along with the oak, Siberian cedar and many others. Himself an experienced gardener, Prior Damascene began the work of laying out magnificent orchards and plantations on the island. In 1866, the monastery orchards had 400 apple trees of 60 different kinds, and the monks managed to grow water-melons and strawberries!

110. In past centuries, when the monastery was Valaam's only lawful master, all hunting there was banned. Animals grew so tame they would wander into hermitages and among monastery buildings. Even now elks, foxes and hares in the protected forests have very little fear of man.

few who managed to hide on the more remote islands. But every time Valaam rose from the ashes, restored to its former splendour.

In the 14th century, Valaam became one of the leading Orthodox centres in the region, and several of its monks founded new monasteries in Karelia and in the Russian North. Among them were Alexander of the Svir, Arseny of Konev, who in 1393 established the Nativity Monastery on the Ladoga island of Konevets, and Sabbatius, one of the founders of the famous Solovetsky Monastery on the White Sea.

The last calamitous devastation of the Valaam Monastery was recorded in 1611, when the cloister was razed to the ground by a Swedish general, Jacob Pontius de la Gardie. Those monks who escaped the slaughter found refuge in St Basil's Monastery by Old Ladoga. Having routed the Swedes and recaptured the Karelian isthmus, Peter the Great issued a special decree in 1715 ordering the restoration of Valaam.

The job of restoring the Valaam Monastery was entrusted to the Cyril-Belozero Monastery, and until 1720 the Saviour Transfiguration Monastery on Valaam remained under St Cyril's. But building activity there was rather slack till 1781, when Metropolitan Gabriel of the Sarov cloister sent a new prior, Nazarius, to the island. That was also the time when the monastery started active missionary work; Valaam monks travelled as far afield as Alaska, and were the first to introduce native Americans to Orthodox Christianity.

The monastery's next palmy period was under Prior Damascene, who took over in 1839. In his time, the rules of monastic life became

111. Only ships specially chartered to bring pilgrims from St Petersburg moor for the night in Great Nikon Bay (overleaf). After a hot day, the straits and bays are enveloped in a pall of mist lit up by the rays of the never-setting sun.

generally more strict, and in several of the Valaam hermitages they were inordinately ascetic. But Prior Damascene's chief passion was building and development. Nicknamed Valaam's Peter the Great, he gave the island its best buildings, designed by A.M. Gornostaev. The cloister, hermitages and harbours were linked by good roads, and canals were cut through the rocks to join the inner lakes to Ladoga.

Damascene also intended to have the island's main church, the Transfiguration Cathedral, rebuilt, but it was his successor, Prior Jonathan, who actually carried out the project. In 1881, in his sixty-third year on Varlaam, Damascene died at the age of eighty-six and was buried in the Prior Cemetery he himself had established.

By 1904, the Valaam Monastery had over a thousand monks and 300,000 rubles in St Petersburg banks. The godliness of Valaam life, the riches of the monastery and the spiritual values it preached were renowned throughout Orthodox Christendom. Valaam became a major pilgrimage centre. In summer it received up to 400 pilgrims a day, and on a more important holiday, such as Transfiguration Day, it could be ten times that number. The annual total reached 40,000. The monastery's reputation and beautiful surroundings attracted several Russian tsars and grand dukes, starting with Alexander I in 1819. From the mid-19th century, the island was a 'summer art class' for many Russian artists—from Ivan Shishkin to Nikolai Roerich. The island was also a source of inspiration for poet Alexander Apukhtin and composer Piotr Tchaikovsky.

After the 1917 revolution, when Finland proclaimed indepen-

112. *The gate to All Saints' Hermitage on Valaam. The hermitage was founded in 1793, but the cathedral it has today was built in 1849-1850. At present this is the summer residence of the Moscow Patriarch, for the Valaam Monastery is under the Patriarchate and its father superior has the title of Representative.*

113. *Fresco in the dome of St George's Church in Old Ladoga. Attributed to the Novgorod school, the 12th-century frescoes in this church are considered some of the earliest genuinely Russian paintings. Since the similar frescoes in the Novgorod Nereditsa Church were lost in the Second World War, these have acquired additional imortance. (See p. 142)*

dence, the Valaam Monastery became part of Finnish territory. Its influence and activity were considerably diminished as a result, and the community was far less numerous, though it remained a major centre of Orthodox Christianity and Russian culture. The winter of 1939-1940 was the monastery's last. When the Soviet-Finnish war broke out, the monks left Valaam, crossing frozen Ladoga on foot and taking with them the most valuable and treasured relics, icons, archives and even bells, to seek refuge in the innermost parts of Finland. There, not far from Heinavesi, they founded the New Valaam Monastery.

The current sorry state of the island buildings is, alas, a product of peacetime. After the Second World War, an invalid home was the island's chief occupant for some thirty years. From lack of proper care, the place fell into decay, the gardens gradually reverted to nature and many of the buildings lay in ruins. The monastery was revived on Valaam only in 1989.

Now there are something like six hundred people living on the island in addition to a modest-sized monastic community.

Cruise vessels coming to Valaam moor in Great Nikon Bay, from where the red brick walls of the Resurrection Hermitage buildings can

114, 115. St George's Church (12th century) in Old Ladoga, the town mentioned in chronicles in connection with the invitation extended to Varangian (Viking) princes in 862 to come and rule over Russia. The building of the church, dedicated to the patron saint of warriors, could have been undertaken in connection with the victory of Ladoga citizens over the Swedes in 1164. The somewhat flattened, helmet-shaped dome is characteristic of old Novgorod architecture. This is one of the smallest of the old Russian churches: its height from floor level to dome is less than 15 metres.

be glimpsed among the pines on the high cliffs. But the usual place to start getting acquainted with the island is Monastery Bay, where tourists are taken by a local motorboat. (Walking enthusiasts can get there on foot along a picturesque road of 6 km.)

During this short trip by motorboat, the dome of a miniature church can be seen peeping above the treetops on a densely wooded isle near the shore. The dome belongs to the Hermitage of St John the Baptist, and the isle is called Predtechensky ('of the Baptist'). The hermitage church, designed by architect A.M. Gornostaev, was built on the isle in 1858.

The next island on the motorboat's way is Skitsky (Hermitage), the second-largest of the Valaam archipelago. Ahead lies St Nicholas's Hermitage and its church (1853), again designed by Gornostaev, tucked away on a smallish island by the left shore of the narrow entrance to Monastery Bay, which forms a deep inlet. Here, nearly a kilometre from the open lake, is the wharf where motorships from Sortavala dock as well. On the ship's left, as it goes through Monastery Bay, three chapels can be seen on the shore. The foremost one, right next to the wharf, is the Annunciation Chapel (late 18th century)

116. St Petersburg on the Neva was founded by Peter the Great as Russia's 'window on the West' in the early 1700s. The spire in the foreground belongs to the Admiralty. Its weather-vane in the form of a little ship has become the symbol of the city, the country's greatest port and for over two centuries its capital.

which, together with the mews and carriage house in its immediate vicinity, is the oldest of the buildings now standing on Valaam.

From the quay, a flight of stone steps up the hillside leads to the main group of monastery buildings. On the top of the hill, left of the steps, stands the Saviour Transfiguration Cathedral, designed by architects G.I. Karpov, A.N. Silin and N.D. Prokofiev (1887-1896). Some of the original frescoes have survived.

The cathedral stands inside a rectangle formed by two blocks of monks' cells. The inner block, built between 1785 and 1801, comprises the earliest brick buildings here, dating back to the time of Prior Nazarius. The northern side of the rectangle is closed by the Assumption Church, consecrated in 1785 and rebuilt in the last century. The outer block was built in stages during the 19th century and completed in the early 1900s. Apart from monks' cells it also housed various workshops.

In the middle of the rectangle's southern side are the Holy Gate surmounted by the Church of St Peter and St Paul, both from 1809. On the same axis with them, but on the opposite side, there formerly stood the 19th-century Church of the Life-Giving Source and the Holy Trinity, destroyed during the Soviet-Finnish war. West of the Holy Gate are the 'tsar's cells', so named after first Alexander I, and then Alexander II, lodged there when visiting the island.

North of the rectangle of cells is the Old Cemetery. Beyond it, on the very edge of the bluff, is the Water House (1860-1864), built by architect Gornostaev, which once housed a steam engine that pumped water from Monastery Bay up a tunnel cut through the rocks. The water was supplied to the various buildings of the monastery, and the engine also powered machines in the nearby workshops.

To the right of the steps, on the other side of the monastery, is the hostel, designed by Gornostaev and built in 1852, which could accommodate up to a thousand visitors, It was constructed following the start of the regular steamer service from St Petersburg, after which the flow of pilgrims increased dramatically. Visitors were given free accommodation and meals at the monastery refectory.

An avenue starting at the main monastery complex leads to the Prior Cemetery, about a kilometre away, where all the priors of the monastery, beginning with Damascene, were buried. The Holy Fathers Church at the cemetery and its belfry were designed by architect G.I. Karpov and built in 1876.

Scattered all over the islands at varying distances from the central complex are hermitages, of which there were thirteen in 1917. These were places where monks seeking greater seclusion went to live in groups of two to thirty. The oldest and biggest was All Saints' Hermitage on Skitsky Island. Founded as early as 1793 by Prior Nazarius, it was rebuilt under Prior Damascene by architects K. Brandt and A.M. Gornostaev. The hermitage's church (1849-1850) is one of Gornostaev's finest creations. Around the church there are eight one-storeyed buildings with monks' cells, the prior's residence, the refectory and various auxiliary rooms.

Above Great Nikon Bay, where cruise vessels moor, is the Resurrection Hermitage. Legend names this part of the island as the place where St Andrew the Apostle raised a cross upon reaching Valaam. The event is commemorated by one of the aisles dedicated to St Andrew in the hermitage church (1901-1906) by architect V.I. Barankeev. Within a kilometre of the Resurrection Hermitage is the Hermitage of Gethsemane, set up in 1911. It consists of the wooden Assumption Church and a small wooden chapel some way off.

Old and New Ladoga. From Valaam the ship sails southwards, towards the source of the Neva, and there are no more stops until it reaches St Petersburg. But there are two towns on the southern shore of Lake Ladoga that it would be a pity to miss if one has set out on a journey to the Land of White Nights. When the ship is heading for St Petersburg from the Svir bypassing Valaam, it goes past the source of the Volkhov, which in days of yore was part of the road 'from the Varangians to the Greeks', and in the 18th and 19th centuries formed part of the Vyshny Volochek navigation system linking the Volga to St Petersburg. There, by the source of the Volkhov, on the highway from St Petersburg to Lodeinoe Pole, stands the town of New Ladoga, founded by Peter the Great in 1704 close to the Monastery of St Nicholas Medvedsky. The two surviving monastery buildings are St Nicholas's Cathedral (15th-16th centuries) and the Church of St John the Evangelist (19th century). The town on the Volkhov bank has preserved the so-called Suvorov Barracks that once belonged to the Suzdal Regiment, commanded in the 1760s by the great General Alexander Suvorov. There is also a monument to Suvorov, put up in 1947, and the small wooden Church of St George, built in 1768 at Suvorov's expense on the southern outskirts of the town.

Twelve kilometres from New Ladoga, along the road on the Volkhov's left bank leading to Volkhovstroi Station, is Old Ladoga, one of the oldest villages in Leningrad Region. Originally known simply as Ladoga, it was the centre of Slavic settlement south of Lake Ladoga as early as the 7th to 9th centuries. Archaeologists excavating an ancient rampart-encircled fortress in Old Ladoga found a birch-bark scroll with a 9th-century drawing on it and the remains of wooden boats. Caches of European and Arab coins found in the area bear witness to Ladoga's importance in the past as a junction of trade routes.

The first mention of Ladoga as a military centre occurs in one of the sagas dating from 997 recorded by Icelandic chronicler Snorri Sturlusson. In 1114, on the recommendation of the Kievan prince, Vladimir Monomakh, a stone fortress was built on the promontory formed by the small Ladozhka River where it flows into the Volkhov. The fortress was rebuilt in the 15th century, after Ladoga became a major trade centre and stronghold in the north-west of Russia.

From 1610 to 1617 Ladoga had to endure Swedish occupation, but following the signing of the Stolbovo Peace Treaty in 1617, it was again incorporated in the Russian lands. In 1701, the fortress withstood the last siege in its history and, with the Great Northern War over, gradually lost its defensive role. After New Ladoga was built and the administration transferred there, the old town languished till it was no more than a village.

One of the four surviving fortress towers, the Gate Tower, houses the museum of Old Ladoga's history. Within the fortress boundaries there is a magnificent monument of Old Russian architecture: the Church of St George from the late 12th century (though some experts believe it dates back to the reign of Yaroslav the Wise, in the first half of the 11th century). The splendid frescoes of St George's are extremely rare examples of 12th-century monumental painting. Next to the Church of St George is the wooden Church of St Demetrius of Salonika, somewhat like a peasant house in appearance. The church, apparently built in the early 17th century and rebuilt in 1731, now contains the ethnography section of the Old Ladoga museum.

Another typical example of Old Russian architecture, along with St George's Church, is the Assumption Cathedral of the Assumption Monastery in Old Ladoga, mentioned for the first time in the 15th century. A number of other buildings in stone have survived from several monasteries founded around Old Ladoga from the 14th to 16th centuries. In St Nicholas's Monastery this is St Nicholas's Cathedral, built in the 17th century on the site of a 12th-century church, and the Church of St John Chrysostom (1860-1862) by architect A.M. Gornostaev, again replacing an earlier church. The only building that remains of St Basil's Monastery is the Church of St Basil the Great from the first decade of the seventeenth century, while the sole relic of the monastery that once crowned Malishev Hill is the Church of St John the Baptist (1695).

Schliesselburg and the Neva. On the left bank of the Neva, where it flows out of Lake Ladoga, stands the town of Schliesselburg (or Petrokrepost, 'Peter's Fortress'). Cruise liners going from Valaam to St Petersburg and back pass the town at night. Any insomniacs among the passengers can get a good view of Schliesselburg from the deck—northern white nights are light enough for that. For those who would like a closer acquaintance with the town, it is just 62 kilometres from St Petersburg up the Neva and 35 kilometres by the Lodeinoe Pole highway. In summer, a hydrofoil takes under two hours to cover the distance between St Petersburg and Schliesselburg.

Across the river, opposite the town, on an island that divides the Neva into two arms, stands the fortress built in 1323 by the Novgorod prince, Yuri Danilovich, who named it Oreshek ('little nut'). In the 16th century the fortress withstood several difficult sieges by the Swedes, but in 1611 the Swedish army captured it and renamed it Noteburg ('nut town' in Swedish). During the Great Northern War, the Russians recaptured the fortress in 1702, and Peter the Great called it Schliesselburg ('key town'), referring to its strategic position. Peter himself designed new fortifications for it. But quite soon the fortress lost its military significance and in the second half of the 18th century was used as a place of confinement for 'enemies of the state'.

The fortress is at present a history museum.

The town itself emerged in the 14th century as a trading borough. In the early 18th century, after the bypass canal was dug along the southern shore of Lake Ladoga, Schliesselburg became an important transport point, and in the middle of the century a number of ship repair shops were set up which eventually developed into the shipbuilding yard that is there today.

In the central part of the town is the Annunciation Church (1764-1795) with a tall bell-tower (52 m.), built on the site where a wooden church stood in the time of Peter the Great. It is somewhat reminiscent of the cathedral in the Peter-Paul Fortress in St Petersburg. In 1957, a monument to Peter I designed by sculptor Mark Antakolsky was put up in the town. With its old canals, bridges, locks and granite-faced embankments, the place has a very distinct character of its own. Formerly these canals and locks were used as a Ladoga bypass by vessels going to the Neva and further to St Petersburg.

The Neva, though quite short (74 km.), is the largest river in the north-west of Russia in terms of water volume, and fifth in Europe, after the Volga, the Danube, the Kama and the Pechora. It is navigable for sea-going vessels, which can enter Ladoga by way of the Neva. The river's deepest point at St Petersburg is 24 metres. Cruise ships soon cover the distance to the city going along the Neva and, their voyage over, dock at the river terminal on the outskirts. From here one can see the distant gleaming spire of the Admiralty, the symbol of the city which is the 'White Nights Capital'.

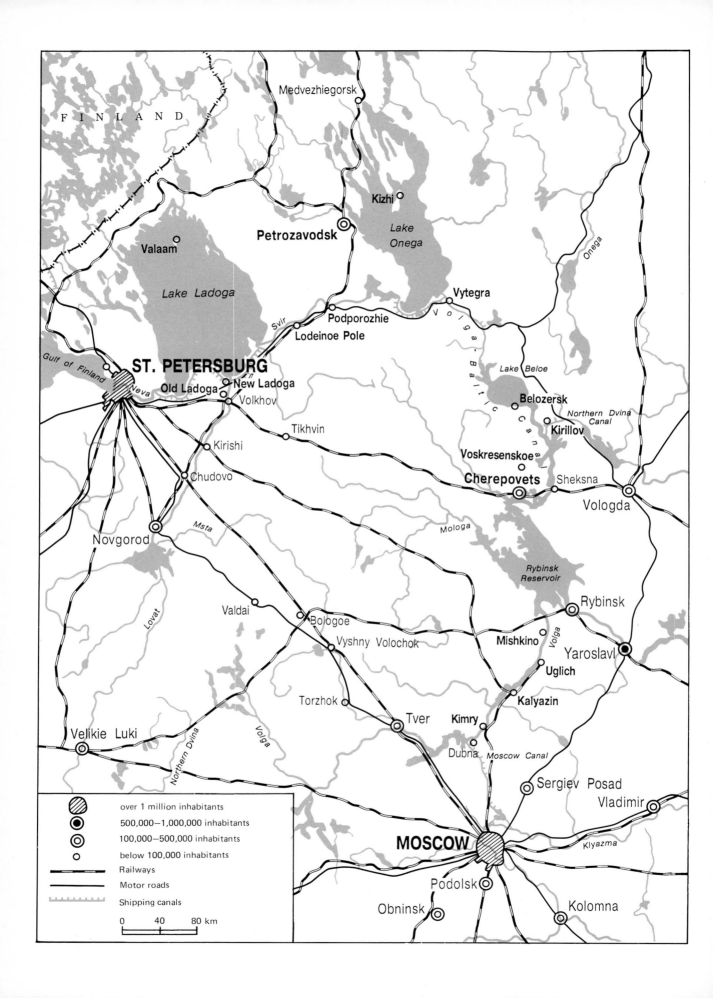

FINLAND

Medvezhiegorsk

Kizhi

Petrozavodsk

Lake Onega

Valaam

Onega

Lake Ladoga

Vytegra

Svir

Podporozhie

Lodeinoe Pole

V o l g a - B a l t i c

Lake Beloe

Gulf of Finland

ST. PETERSBURG

Old Ladoga   New Ladoga

Neva

Volkhov

Tikhvin

Belozersk

Northern Dvina Canal

Kirillov

Kirishi

C a n a l

Chudovo

Voskresenskoe

Cherepovets

Sheksna

Vologda

Msta

Novgorod

Mologa

Rybinsk Reservoir

Valdai

Lovat

Bologoe

Vyshny Volochok

Rybinsk

Mishkino

Volga

Yaroslavl

Uglich

Torzhok

Kalyazin

Velikie Luki

Northern Dvina

Volga

Tver

Kimry

Dubna

Moscow Canal

Sergiev Posad

Vladimir

MOSCOW

Klyazma

over 1 million inhabitants

500,000–1,000,000 inhabitants

100,000–500,000 inhabitants

below 100,000 inhabitants

Railways

Motor roads

Shipping canals

0   40   80 km

Podolsk

Obninsk

Kolomna